NYITVA
GEÖFFNET
OPEN

RESTAURANT OF DAYS GONE BY

PUBLISHED BY YESTERDAY AND TODAY CULTURAL FOUNDATION

BUDAPEST, 1995

TEGNAP ÉS MA ALAPÍTVÁNY

Published for the
Yesterday and Today Cultural Foundation
by INTENT Ltd.

Executive publisher: Pál Traub

Editor: Ágnes Tóth

Editing assistants:
Dr. Katalin Csapó, Dr. Balázs Draveczky
Dr. Thománé Éva Nagyváthy, Judit Varga

Photographs and reproductions: Péter Korniss

Design: Zoltán Kemény

English translation: Elayne M. Antalffy

The archive materials used as illustrations
were placed at the disposal of the publisher
by the Buda Private Museum Foundation,
the Kiscelli Museum of the Budapest History Museum,
and the Museum of Hungarian Commerce and Catering.

ISBN 963 04 59264

Prepared for printing by: Csaba László / Gráfium
Printed by: Alföldi Nyomda
Executive director: Géza György

Budapest 1995

"In those days Pest had the smell of imperial rolls, fresh draught beer and Wiener sausages. (I once wrote somewhere about the smells of different cities. I observed in Vienna, for example, that although more beer and Wiener sausages are sold there than in Pest, the city has the smell of fruit and antique shops. Or rather, it used to have.) Even in the summer flow of the gutters, in old Pest the traveller caught a whiff of the special Pest smell that was not unpleasant. The smell of the Pest inns even filtered through the Christmas tree-scented winter snowfalls. The steams from beer-houses in the side streets overwhelmed the smells from the silk and leather merchants' shops in the inner city. The atmosphere of the inns where travellers had just pulled into the court in a carriage equalled the bazaar, sawdust and canvas smell of Kerepesi Road. Józsefváros had an odour of fresh cooked sausage and fresh cabbage; while Ferencváros was a big wine cellar, where the old citizens had faces the colour of rosé wine, people sang in the courtyards of inns and geraniums blushed in the windows. Buda in winter had the smell of an old church after litany. In summer oniony fish soup vied with the almond and sugary flavours of the vendor's basket-tray.

The streets of Pest were full of smells that tickled the imagination. Around the bakery shops, engulfed in the smell of freshly baked pastries, it was easy to imagine the fair-haired, grey-eyed young lady reading a novel in the silence of the bakery shop.

Arriving in Pest: it was a joyful and glorious morning. Pest, freshly washed and cheerful, awaited the traveller emerging from the sooty air of the railway stations.

The waiter's freshly pressed jacket, the sprinkled streets, the tempting freshness of the shops, the brightness of the roofs, the unpleasant bustle of big city life lulled the traveller into the dream of a happy, youthful city. How the Danube sparkled! And what shining shoes the people of society wore on the promenade! The faces, the people, clothes, moods were as fresh every day as the breakfast rolls."

Gyula Krúdy: A visit to Pest

ELŐSZÓ

VORWORT

FOREWORD

Only those who have reached a ripe old age and lived a respected life have found a place in this book.

There have been thousands of outstanding businesses in the history of catering in Budapest – legendary hotels, prestigious restaurants, small inns famous for their cooking, coffee-houses providing a home for writers, poets and prima donnas, confectioners' shops that became known throughout the world and bars that are a mine of unforgettable stories. It has not been our intention to write the history of catering once again – this has already been done by many others – but rather to bring the reader a collection of a kind that is almost certainly unique.

Many famous restaurateurs lost their lives on the front during the two world wars and during World War II many buildings housing renowned restaurants and hotels were destroyed in the bombing raids and then in the fighting from street to street. The once splendid row of hotels beside the Danube was practically razed and what was left of it – a couch draped with a Persian rug, a Venetian mirror, a table beer-warmer or a graceful silver jug – was looted by people who defied even martial law.

A few dynasties of restaurateurs – such as the Gundel or the Auguszt families – survived all this. But no sooner had they recovered and set up business again than they lost everything again. Nationalisation began soon after the end of World War II and was eventually extended even to the smaller businesses. For decades the hotels, restaurants and confectioners' shops were in state ownership – imposing a drab uniformity on them all. The bars and coffee-houses, as "middle-class places", were closed down and often "people's restaurants" for catering on a mass scale were opened in their place.

Those Budapest catering places which survived even this and once again created their former splendour, and others where a quality business is once again operating on the old site have been included in this album. There are also many beautiful old photographs of buildings, signboards, businesses, old implements used for cooking, baking and serving, fancy menu cards, and of course, the guests and the restaurateurs themselves, evoking the atmosphere of the turn of the century. We also cast a glimpse at their appearance today.

We have included a few of the more important places which in one way or another were destroyed or ceased to exist, but which were once well known and popular. A separate short chapter is devoted to these.

All this clearly shows the intention of the Foundation and the Publishing House: to entertain and delight those who like to immerse themselves in the past, who feel an affinity to literature, poetry, painting and acting, because the history of catering in Budapest is also in a way the unofficial history of the arts in our city. Since some of the hotels, restaurants and especially the coffee-houses gained real fame because they were the favourite haunts of artists, the illustrations have been supplemented with extracts from works by outstanding Hungarian writers and poets during this period of close to a hundred years. Naturally, we have selected passages relevant to their gastronomic experiences or life in the coffee-houses. The reader will also find anecdotes written by journalists or even by the great figures of catering, and there are also a few contemporary descriptions of how dishes were made.

We are able to bring all this to the reader because, besides placing valuable documents at our disposal, the Museum of Hungarian Commerce and Catering has assisted the production of this volume with a wealth of information and advice. We express our gratitude to all the staff of the Museum.

The Editor

ROYAL ORFEUM
OPERETTE

"How charming it used to be to see the old shop sign-boards on Rákóczi Street, to drive by the familiar restaurants and coffee-houses and know for certain who was sitting in them and where, to see in one's imagination the tables reserved for regular guests in the Metropole, the neat dining-rooms of the Pannónia, the acquaintances drinking black coffee in the Balaton, the regulars of the Hungária and all the other people of Pest, whose habits, way of sitting, luncheons and amusements we knew as precisely as the calendar. Do not try to find them on the old chairs, at the old tables. Strangers are sitting there, people you have never seen."

Gyula Krúdy: A visit to Pest

Ferenc Szikszay's restaurant, 1890s

"Well, János, when I was police captain in Szatmár, I became accustomed to not eating when the bells in the towers rang soup-time at noon, but whenever I could find the time. As a result, my stomach is not like other people's stomachs. Right now, for example, I feel like a bit of something left over from luncheon. Just a small helping of Székely goulash, say. Or a wee bit of pörkölt, but with plenty of fat and gravy. I wouldn't mind if there was a bit of goulash in the kitchen left over from this morning, of course, with bones and meat, topped up with a little meat soup, a few vegetables and perhaps a scrap of bone marrow. Just don't offer me lights János, because that's only good when it's fresh.

– We'll serve you some goulash soup in a plate then!

– In a soup bowl, so that I can't see Szikszay's monogram for the soup – says Pátri who for some reason seems to harbour such a grudge against old Szikszay, the former owner, that he does not wish to see even his monogram on the edge of the plate."

Gyula Krúdy: The man with an enormous appetite, or how Pátri ate to his fill in Pest

Menu, 1938

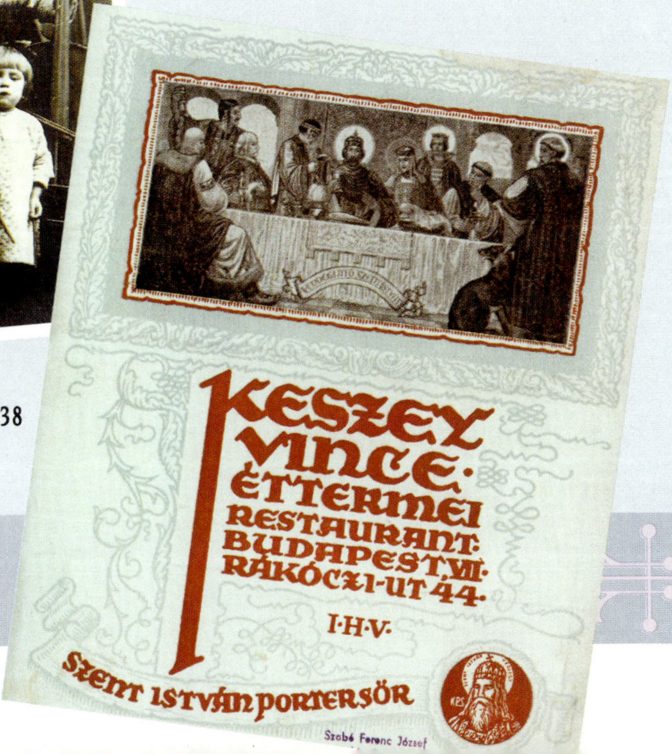

Béla Drechsler's restaurant, around 1902

Menu, 1902

..."The Geranium Table Society comprising singers, artists and journalists flourished in the restaurant from 1906 to 1910, at times in the cellar, at other times on the ground floor. Leoncavallo, Mascagni, Puccini and Ibsen were visitors here. And just as the king washes the feet of a few old people from Buda in the church each year, so Goldmark and Mahler obeyed with a smile when the coffee-grinder was pressed into their hands for them to assist at the table's speciality, the ceremony of coffee-making."...

Imre Gundel – Judit Harmath:
Memoirs of Catering

István Frenreisz's restaurant, around 1910

Menu, 1906

Menu, 1929

Virágbokor restaurant, around 1910

Beer tankard, 1870s

Kiosk on Gellért Hill, around 1909

"Who could possibly list all the little inns in Buda with mulberry and walnut trees, oleanders and geraniums where they served the droves of guests chicken pörkölt, with freshly made noodles, peppery cabbage strudel with pastry rolled out paper-thin, carefully rolled up and soaked in sour cream, and all the pleasant dishes, equally kind to palate and stomach, accompanied by red or white wine that the waiter brought not in a crystal glass but an earthenware jug, or by a mug of foaming, fresh draught beer, while the fruit came straight from the ice, black coffee was made in a glass boiling flask and anyone who wished was given a finger-bowl and white hand-towel with the solo crab caught in Zala."

Sándor Lestyán: Little inns, summer outdoor restaurants

Hubertus wine tavern and bistro, 1935

1910

Japán coffee-house, around 1930

"We used to have a coffee-house on Andrássy Road in those more congenial days: the Japan Coffee-house. Its white majolica walls were all painted with bamboo, chrysanthemums, vases, imaginary birds. – The coffee-house is still open: time has been closed. – Those of us who frequented the Japan perhaps went even further than if we had gone to Japan. This coffee-house was more remotely exotic than the world of the white lotus, green tea and golden Buddha, because the Japan Coffee-house was the home of the fairy of youth."

Speech made by Ernő Szép at the commemorative session of the Szinyei Academy, 1931

Carte Postale – To the artists – Japan Coffee-House – Andrássy Road – Budapest
My oriental journey has been fully successful. – If Szinyei or Dr. Lázár are present, I request them to communicate this to the government and the public. I shall be with you in a few days.
Constantinople, 29 Sept. 1913

Csontváry

Japán coffee-house, around 1910 (The man with the grey beard is Pál Szinyei Merse and the man in the hat, second from right, is József Rippl Rónai, both famous painters)

Negresco coffee-house, late 1920s

Baross coffee-house, early 1900s

Waitresses at the turn of the century

Bodó coffee-house, around 1912

Mikszáth coffee-house, around 1914

Central coffee-house, 1909

"Who remembers when even the dogs drank real French champagne if a member of the country gentry came up to Pest to deliver his tobacco harvest, when the stove lad swept up great shards of shattered mirror from the floor of the coffee-house towards dawn, when rubber-wheeled carriages bearing laughing, merry women and gallants sped along Stefánia Road after a night of revelry to take them to the little pubs in City Park for a glass of cold beer?...
Who remembers all these delights?"

István Bródy: Who remembers?

Abbázia coffee-house, 1901

"He went into the coffee-house for that piccolo coffee and the appearance of that coffee-cup on his table reflected the life, fate and political allegiance of the citizen of Pest. This piccolo coffee gave news of the citizen's temperament, depending on when and in which coffee-house he drank it: a black coffee sipped after lunch in the Abbázia shows that the citizen has plans for disrupting the city, he has a tendency to more liberal thoughts, he is uneasy for some reason even though there seems to be no problem in the city.

A piccolo taken in the neighbourhood of the stock exchange has a different symbolism from one in the New York coffee-house late at night. In the former, members of the stock exchange appear to conduct their transactions, they leave with wads of banknotes wrapped in newspapers, and it is here that toilers bring their wads while in the New York, late at night, the piccolo coffee is a certain sign that the coffee-drinker is conducting a secret affair with the stage or with literature.

In the final analysis, it could be said that it was enough to ask the citizen of old Pest to which coffee-house he had his mail addressed and within minutes one would have a clear picture of his society, ideals and view of the world."

Gyula Krúdy: The story of X.Y., democrat from Pest and genuine citizen

Menu, 1930

Spolarich coffee-house, around 1913

"There are also people in Pest who do not like coffee-houses; they prefer to frequent confectioners' shops.

I do not mean privileged persons who are regulars at Gerbeaud, Lukács, Flóris or August, but the bourgeois, solid middle-class ladies who are great lovers of sweets. Men are not as frequent guests in these places as are the ladies. Men opt for confectioners' shops for the sake of the ladies. A little flirt, a little harmless chat – nothing more.

Those who cannot afford theatres or cinemas are happy in the confectioners' shops, the world of silent but eloquent handclasps, soft sighs, apple tarts, cream cakes and meringues.

The foundation-stone of many a romantic novel and an ideal marriage has been laid in these sweet places."

István Bródy:
Entertainment in today's Pest

Gerbeaud pavilion, 1912

Emil Szavanov's confectioner's shop, 1920s

Ravasz confectionery, 1916

Advertisement from the 1910s

Bonbon box 1910s

Miss Arizona

"There is no need for any special introduction. For two years now we have seen her every evening in the little bonbonnière. The magic of her performance has even won the most demanding public of Pest. With her inimitable charm, her light, warm voice, she wins a place in people's hearts...

Everyone who counts at all in Pest can be found in the boxes. They come to see the show, because everyone is talking about it and everyone has to have something to say about it.

Young aristocrats can be found here, just as the cream of the business world. They come here as though they were going home. This is their home...

The new programme it presents its public is the peak of the Arizona's popularity. Sándor Rozsnyai's imaginative management has made the little bar a tourist attraction. This can be seen in the fact that anyone who visits Pest, whether it be the Prince of Wales or anyone else, first heads for the Arizona."

Pest Courier, 1935

Arizona bar,
early 1940s and around 1932

Programme, 1937 and 1938

Royal Orfeum, 1910s

Programme, 1925

"American millionaires, foreign diplomats, aristocrats, film stars, famous writers and artists, sojourning in Pest, visited these places one by one, and their enthusiastic declarations justified the existence of the refined and elegant entertainment places which, we may say, really did become strong pillars of tourism in Hungary.

The real image of Pest, which is now beautiful, can be seen to perfection when the arc lamps open their big, curious eyes, when the gold-braided doormen of these new fairy palaces salute the clients arriving at the doors in shining automobiles, opening the door for the people who seek entertainment and amusement – for those who have the means to live by night – and sleep by day."

István Bródy: The golden age of bars

Fővárosi Orfeum, around 1910

Moulin Rouge, around 1932

Winter premises of the Parisien Grill, around 1930

"This bar brought an entirely new colour and style to night-life. The greatest significance of the Parisien Grill was that it made Pest night-life socially acceptable. Before that, although the posters declared that the refined public danced on the parquet, in fact, only the dancing girls and dancers hired by the place, and one or two young men shuffled on the parquet. The Grill was the bar where countesses and the ladies of financial magnates danced till dawn. The Grill was the first entertainment place that was also frequented by countesses."

István Bródy: The golden age of bars

Summer premises of the Parisien Grill, around 1930

István Főherczeg Hotel, end of the 1890s

Budapest 1897 atv. 11.

A csütörtöki asztaltársaság által

MÁRKUS JÓZSEF Főpolgármester

HALMOS JÁNOS Polgármester

TISZTELETÉRE RENDEZETT DISZLAKOMA

Étrendje

Hors d'oeuvre à la Russe

Potage

Consommé de volaille en tasses

Poisson

Fogas à la Hongroise

Rélevée

Filet de boeuf à la surprise

Entrée

Chaudfroid de faisan en plumage

Rôts

Poularde de Styrie et Canetons

Salade Italienne

Compote assortie

Entremets

Parfait le „Triomphe"

Patisseries Fruits Fromage

Café

Vins: Ménesi 1881, Magyarádi 1887

Champ.: Moët & Chandon cremant rosée

GUNDEL JÁNOS „István főherczeg" szállodája.

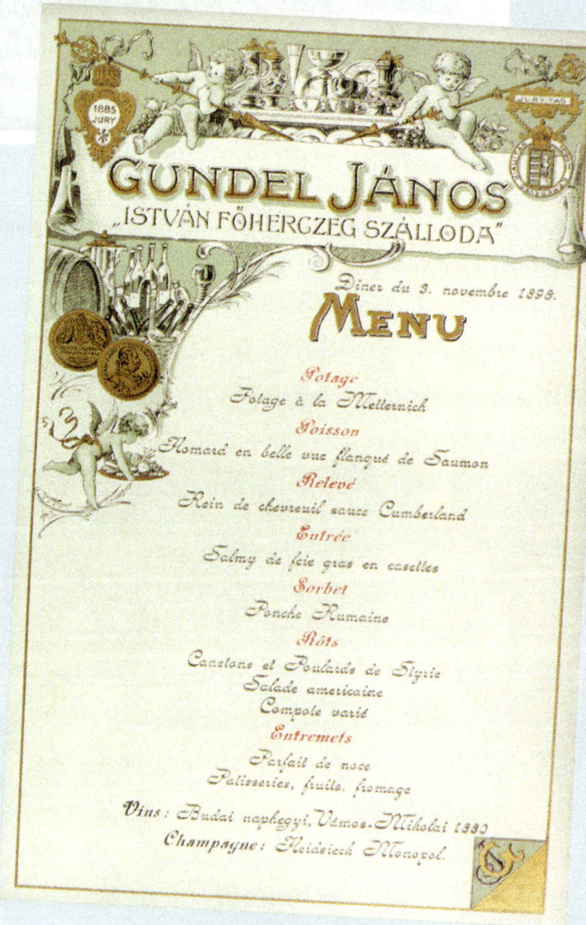
GUNDEL JÁNOS

„ISTVÁN FŐHERCZEG SZÁLLODA"

Diner du 3. novembre 1898.

MENU

Potage

Potage à la Metternich

Poisson

Homard en belle vue flanqué de Saumon

Relevé

Rein de chevreuil sauce Cumberland

Entrée

Salmy de foie gras en caselles

Sorbet

Ponche Rumaine

Rôts

Canetons et Poulards de Styrie

Salade americaine

Compote varié

Entremets

Parfait de noce

Patisseries, fruits, fromage

Vins: Budai naphegyi, Vámos-Mikolai 1880

Champagne: Heidsieck Monopol.

Menus

Advertisement from the late 1840s

"This splendid dish does not come from the Palóc region. It was created in Pest, next door to the Academy, in what was once the patriarchal Archduke Stephen Hotel (István főherceg Szálloda)...
... The first Palóc soup was made in 1892, in honour of Kálmán Mikszáth, the "great Palóc", who was a great connoisseur and understood and appreciated good food and drink. He used to go with his friends and fellow writers, with members of the Kisfaludy Society and others, to the famous private room in the Archduke Stephen.

Mr. János Gundel, a charming and interesting figure, the genius restaurateur... created the new dish, Palóc soup, to give pleasure to his well loved guests...
... there are no devilish tricks about the recipe. Begin as though it were a pörkölt. Heat a spoonful of lard in a wide and sufficiently deep pan, fry a grated onion in it, and sprinkle on a teaspoon of sweet Szeged paprika. Add a kilogramme of diced tender leg (or even better, shoulder) of well-fed mutton and brown together with a few crushed caraway seeds. In the meantime, in separate pans cook half a kilogramme of diced potatoes and the same quantity of sliced and carefully stringed green beans, in salt water (or if you prefer, in bone, meat or vegetable stock). Pour these, without straining, together with a few bayleaves, over the browned meat, using only as much of their liquid as required to give the new soup the thickness of a good goulash. Bring to the boil and if the other ingredients, as well as the meat are tender, stir in two or three decilitres of good, rich sour cream to bring the harmony of its excellent flavours and aromas to the peak of perfection. It is then ready to serve to appreciative friends who are close to one's heart. For only one's best friends are worthy of this sublime Hungarian dish."

Elek Magyar: The Gourmet's Cookbook

Vadászkürt Hotel, around 1934

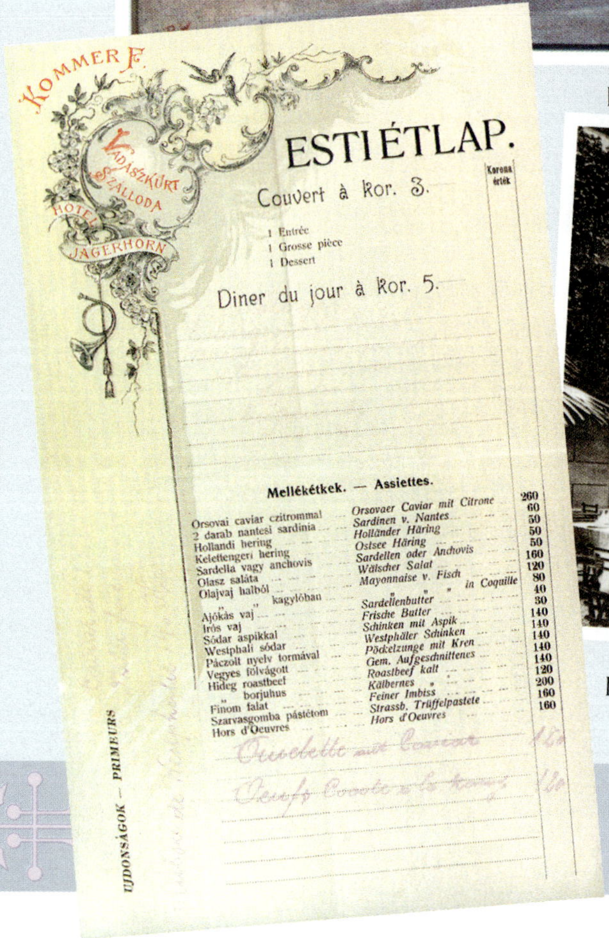

KOMMER F.

VADÁSZKÜRT SZÁLLODA

HOTEL JÄGERHORN

ESTIÉTLAP.

Couvert à kor. 3.

1 Entrée
1 Grosse pièce
1 Dessert

Diner du jour à kor. 5.

Korona érték

Mellékétkek. — Assiettes.

Orsovai caviar czitrommal	Orsovaer Caviar mit Citrone	260
2 darab nantesi sardinia	Sardinen v. Nantes	60
Hollandi hering	Holländer Häring	50
Keletengeri hering	Ostsee Häring	50
Sardella vagy anchovis	Sardellen oder Anchovis	50
Olasz saláta	Wälscher Salat	160
Olajvaj halból	Mayonnaise v. Fisch	120
" kagylóban	" " " in Coquille	80
Ajókás vaj	Sardellenbutter	40
Irós vaj	Frische Butter	30
Sódar aspikkal	Schinken mit Aspik	140
Westphali sódar	Westphäler Schinken	140
Páczolt nyelv tormával	Pöckelzunge mit Kren	140
Vegyes fölvágott	Gem. Aufgeschnittenes	140
Hideg roastbeef	Roastbeef kalt	140
" borjuhus	Kälbernes "	120
Finom falat	Feiner Imbiss	200
Szarvasgomba pástétom	Strassb. Trüffelpastete	160
Hors d'Oeuvres	Hors d'Oeuvres	160

ÚJDONSÁGOK – PRIMEURS

Pálmakert, 1910s

Menu, 1900

"A building has been erected here on Elizabeth Boulevard, on a giant scale, with three enormous wings, at a cost of two and a half million forints. In the evening its electric lights are lit and cast their shining white light far along the dark boulevard. A fountain gurgles in the court and tiny, intimate terraces look out onto the street, white statues rise above patches of greenery, thick-piled carpets muffle the sound of footsteps and there is heavy silk, damask and brocade everywhere...

... Do not for a minute think, gentle reader, as you turn these pages, that I am telling a tale about a fairy castle. Or if I am, it is not a castle deep in the magic forest, but a modern fairy palace with three lifts. This fairy mansion has been set for the millennium as a pearl in the splendid string we call the boulevard, to the delight of all who have seen it. But is there anyone who has not? Hotel Royal has become such an attraction of Budapest that the guide-books have given it three stars, like a good cognac."

Jenő Heltai: Hotel Royal

Magyar Király Hotel, 1861

Hét Választó Fejedelem Inn, advertisement for a concert, 1829

Hotel Royal, around 1930

"Indeed, the famous inn was only a two-storey, long, square house... the rain had long ago washed the plaster off its walls and wiped all traces of the black paint off its window-frames. A shingled coach-house for carriages, carts and horses stood in its big unpaved yard. Along the front, upstairs were the rooms for guests, spacious rooms with white stucco and giant brick stoves, yellow beds of softwood with clean, bright covers. On the wall reflecting shades polished mirror-smooth stood proudly behind the tallow candles with red wicks; the tinder was kept in a small lead container beside them, together with a scrap of yellow sulphur strip so that the guest could strike a light."

Lajos Hatvany: The old innkeeper and his son, the bungler

Thirty-one
stories about renowned restaurants, confectioners' shops and hotels operating in Budapest today, which were established in the mid-nineteenth century or around the early years of the twentieth century.

"We feed to love – I still hold by this axiom. However, I am beginning to understand the opposite fundamental truth too, and I am coming to see that eating could also be regarded as an end in itself. Eating with feeling, sensually, with imagination, with passionate love. Before and after great disillusionments – I have been in such a state myself...

But let us put aside philosophy and hasten to pörkölt. This is the chief dish of we who live in this state, whether we be the descendants of the heroic Árpád or of David with his sling. Good, strong, spicy pörkölt – for ever! All parties unite in this belief. There is no difference of opinion, taste or interest in this matter...

You, pörkölt, are best suited to our national character and our climate. But you must be really singed, not wan, pale or light. You must be burning brown and your liquid must be neither too little nor too much, nor too thin either. And if you are made from veal on the bone, you should have a little finely chopped, one could say minced, beef, if possible firm and well coloured rump, to give strength to your liquor...

My recipe is the old and only one, a recipe that cannot be recommended enough."

Sándor Bródy: On the subject of pörkölt

Established: before 1831 *V. Pesti Barnabás utca 2*

Buda Városához vendéglő

SZÁZÉVES ÉTTEREM

The Hundred-Year-Old Restaurant is much older than a hundred years. It was given its present name when it celebrated its centenary: in 1931. A century earlier, in 1831 there was certainly already a restaurant on the ground floor of the genuine Baroque house built in 1755-60, which is why this year is officially recorded as the date of establishment. The immediate predecessor of the Hundred-Year-Old Restaurant was also known as the Hasslinger inn and, although it was located in the heart of the Inner City on the Pest side, its sign-board bore the inscription: To the City of Buda.

No one knows exactly when the first inn was opened on this site. There are writers who hold that some time towards the end of the 18th century boatmen used to drink in the taproom of the house only a few steps from the Danube. What is almost certain is that the Krist family or, more precisely, three successive generations of the family, ran the business which was first called To the City of Buda, then the White Ship, then the Kriszt, and from 1923 once again bore the name of City of Buda.

The oldest pieces of the present furnishings - the carved counter, the Transylvanian stove and the coloured juke-box - were made some time in the early 19th century, and the more recent items were added on the centenary in 1931. This was when the prestigious restaurant was given the name of Hundred-Year-Old.

Heading of a menu, 1944

1910s

Százéves restaurant, 1995

"One of the most popular dishes in the Hasslinger restaurant was »beer soup«. In his National Recipe Book published in 1846, Ferenc Zelena gives the recipe for it as follows: »Boil three pints of beer with cinnamon, lemon-peel and sufficient sugar to sweeten. Place the yolks of 8 eggs in a pan, add half a pint of sour cream brought to the boil, and very slowly whisk them together, then pour the beer over the mixture. Whisk once again and serve on fingers of toasted bread roll.«

... we have almost forgotten Mrs. Krist who was generally addressed as »Aunt Pepi«. She was famous for her stuffed cabbage and her cold specialities, such as the jellied pork brawn she made herself, the jellied meat and cold sausages with mustard. The pork flank stuffed with all kinds of delicious things and richly spiced, with which Mr. Krist's wines went so well, was often mentioned as Aunt Pepi's 'invention'..."

György Galla: The oldest restaurant in Pest

Established: 1838

II. Hűvösvölgyi út 207

Balázs vendéglő

Although there is no written trace of it, the great names of the catering profession claim that there was already an inn known as the Balázs on the site at the end of the 18th century. There are, however, documents to show that a restaurant has operated here since 1838, called Balázs and later the Hűvösvölgy Great Restaurant. At first, only drinks were served, later a few snacks to go with them, and towards the end of the 19th century hot dishes were also added to the menu. From the day of establishment until nationalisation in the late 1940s, six generations of the Balázs family ran the restaurant.

It was almost certainly given the name of Hűvösvölgy Great Restaurant because the popular Buda excursion spot which was, and still exists, in the vicinity of the restaurant, was known as Hűvösvölgy Common. It is accessible by tram, and middle-class families from Pest, as well as members of workers' choral societies, came out from the city to drink a glass of beer in the spacious outdoor restaurant tucked in between forest-clad hills.

The restaurant was burnt down in 1979 but shortly restored to its original form.

1901

1921

"I have read somewhere that a recent American postal affairs minister was in the habit of cooking chicken paprikás in his office. No doubt even with this little occupation on the side, postal affairs in the United States were in the utmost order. It is quite another matter though, whether the chicken paprikás the minister cooked in the office was in order.

... But successful as it was, how much more successful it would have been if the gourmet minister had known what ingredients are needed for a genuine, delicious Hungarian chicken paprikás! That first of all, it requires a young, but already quite plump, freshly killed and dressed Hungarian chicken, cut into 8-10 pieces, washed and dried with a cloth. The preparation must then continue as follows (for two chickens): melt 120-150 g diced smoked bacon, when hot fry a small grated onion in the fat, sprinkle with a good teaspoonful of sweet Szeged paprika, heat again, then add the chicken pieces, salt, and when juices have been reduced brown slightly, then add 1-2 tablespoons of bone stock, cover and braise until tender. Of course, the chicken must be turned occasionally while cooking, and when it is nearly tender, add the liver. Braise with the liver for another 10 minutes or so, then add around 3 decilitres of the best quality, sweet sour cream, heat to boiling point once again and serve at once on a heated serving dish."

Elek Magyar: The Gourmet's Cookbook

GASTSTÄTTEN

RESTAURANTS

Balázs restaurant, 1995

"I can sing of a whole invasion of foreign dishes. How coffee squeezed out good cold bacon. How beefsteak conquered vast territories and then split into different nations, eventually gaining power in the form of filet de boeuf, then as rumpsteak or entrecôte. The respectable old braised meats and veal slices huddle modestly somewhere at the back of the menu. Poor, outmoded notabilities! The noodles, doughnuts and marzipans are still standing, but somewhat uncertainly. The parfaits camp has already sounded the battle horn and they are advancing in different colours and flavours, to oust the natives from the positions they have held for centuries. Their fancy, sophisticated exterior easily conquers palates too."

Kálmán Mikszáth: Hungarian cuisine – Chatter –

Established: around 1860

I. Márvány u. 6

Márványmenyasszony vendéglő

MÁRVÁNYMENYASSZONY ÉTTEREM

The little one-storey house in Krisztinaváros with a cellar built in 1793, where the Sulzbergers, famous wine-growers in the early 19th century later opened a wine tavern, became one of Buda's romantic little restaurants, shaded by large horse chestnut trees. The business later became a restaurant and in the 1880s passed into the ownership of Vilmos Wagner. He had the statue of the Marble Bride erected in the restaurant which he managed until 1904 when he acquired the Terézváros Pilsen Beer Hall. His successor, Gyula Boros, ran the Marble Bride for more than three decades, right up until the Second World War.
The fact that no major alterations have been made to the building which has preserved its old-world atmosphere since 1872 attests to the skill and taste of the old craftsmen

Signboard from the 1910s

Menu, 1905

Signboard (painted shutter), 1919

Márványmenyasszony restaurant, 1995

"... Gypsy orchestras playing verbunk music...popular songs in folk-style by song-writers... created the pleasant atmosphere that went with good food... Lóránd Fráter, a captain of the hussars who composed songs, ordered »a hundred candles« for his table in the Marble Bride; on another occasion the old walls resounded to the voice of Lujza Blaha, the »nightingale of the nation«..."

The famous little restaurant in Márvány Street

Established: 1871

V. Vigadó tér 3

Pilseni Sörcsarnok

MARCO POLO ÉTTEREM

The house was built by the Thonet brothers and designed by the same architects – Antal Szkalnitzky and Henrik Koch jr. – who had designed the Grand Hotel Hungária. There was a restaurant (Pilsner Hall und Restaurant) and coffee-house on the ground floor.

The name remained unchanged for over sixty years, from the foundation in 1871 until the end of the Second World War, but the lease-holders changed frequently. For the most part the establishment was operated by well known and respected restaurateurs, in chronological order: Vilmos Löffelmann, József Petanovics, Béla Nemény and then Ede Keresztes. They all had to face competition because numerous catering places tempted strollers in Vigadó Square and the vicinity. The square was an extension of the famous Pest corso where on summer afternoons elegantly dressed ladies with parasols accompanied by gentlemen with walking sticks strolled up and down, the couples were often followed by children with wooden hoops. The crowds on the promenade formed part of the Pilsen Beer Hall's clientele as well.

For forty years the former beer hall was not used as a restaurant, then in 1989 a luxury Italian restaurant was opened here. It is in Italian ownership at present too, under the name of Marco Polo.

Around 1904

1907

Marco Polo restaurant, 1995

1930

Established: 1877

V. Ferenciek tere 4–8

Holzwarth vendéglő

KÁRPÁTIA ÉTTEREM

The house with a passage-way built by the Franciscans on the site of their former monastery near the Pest side of Elisabeth Bridge was completed in 1877. One of the business premises on the ground floor was leased by Gy^rgy Holzwarth who opened a restaurant there, entrusting its management to Károly Csalányi. The establishment became famous for its Munich beer and luncheon, and the public still called it the Csalányi when – around the turn of the century – it was in the hands of Géza Neusiedler.

In 1925 the restaurant was taken over by the Spolarich family who were widely known in the trade, and operated other restaurants and coffee-houses in the city. The family had the premises altered which were leased by László Károlyi in 1934. Károlyi added new dishes to the menu and named the restaurant Kárpátia (Carpathians), the name which has survived up to this day. After restoration in 1979 the Kárpátia has continued to be one of Budapest's restaurants renowned for its cuisine.

1927

Cover and page of a menu, 1906

Mellékétkek. — Assietten.

		kr.	fill.
Strassburgi libamáj-pástétom	Strassburger Gansleber-Pastete	70	140
2 drb szardinia	2 Stück Sardinien	24	48
2 " anchovis	2 " Anchovies	5	10
1 " keletengeri hering	1 " Ostsee-Häring	22	44
2 " bouillon-hering	2 " Bouillon-Häring	30	60
1 " orosz szardinia	1 " Russen	8	16
Angolna-hal	Aalfisch	35	70
Olasz saláta	Wällischer Salat	60	120
1/2 hollandi hering körítve	1/2 Holländer Häring garnirt	25	50
Ajóka eczettel és olajjal	Sardellen mit Essig und Oel	20	40
Kaviár czitrommal	Caviar mit Citrone	60	120
Orsovai kaviár	Orsovaer Caviar	60	120
Mayonnaise halból	Mayonnaise vom Fisch	35	70
" en coquille	" en coquille	70	140
Finom fölszeletelt	Feiner Imbiss	40	80
Sódar aspikkal	Schinken mit Aspik	65	130
Páczolt nyelv kicsiny	Pöckelzunge mit Kren klein	50	100
Borjustilt	Kalbsbraten	40	80
1/2 sertésnyelv tormával	1/2 Schweinszunge mit Kren	35	70
Veronai szalámi	Veroneser Salami	20	40
Párisi kolbász eczet és olajjal	Pariser mit Essig und Oel	50	100
Hideg felvágott	Kaltes Aufgeschnittenes	25	50
Kanapée	Kanapée	20	40
Sódar-zsemlye	Schinken-Semmel	12	24
Irós-vaj	Frische Butter	15	30
Ajóka-vaj	Sardellen-Butter	25	50
Hideg roastbeef tatár-mártással	Kalter Roastbeef mit Tartar-Sauce	70	140

Halak. — Fische.

		kr.	fill.
Fogas vajjal	Fogas mit Butter	75	150
" olajvajjal	" Mayonnaise		
" kirántva	" gebacken	60	120
Viza sülve	Hausen gebraten	75	150
Toktatármárt. kis 50 kr. 100 f., nagy 75 kr. 150 f.	Dick à la tartare klein 50 kr. 100 Hell., gross		
Kecsege nagyság szerint	Stirl nach Grösse		
Ponty kirántva	Karpfen gebacken	60	120
Csuka ajókával	Hecht mit Sardellen	50	100
Dunapisztráng sülve	Donauforelle gebraten	70	140

Rögtönös étkek. — Speisen à la Minut.

		kr.	fill.
Chateaubriand	Chateaubriand	200	400
Beefsteak	Beefsteak	80	160
" tojással	" mit Ei	90	180
" körözve	" garnirt	100	200
Rumsteak	Rumsteak	100	200
Borjusteak tojáss.	Kalbsteak mit Ei	85	170
Borju-szelet	Kalbs-Schnitzel		
czitrommal	mit Citrone	60	120
Filetdeboeuf saute	Filetdeboeuf saute	80	160
Borju-cotelette	Kalbscotelette, natur.	70	140
Borju-escalop	Escalopp von Kalb	60	120
Rostélyos hagym.	Rostbraten mit Zwiebel	60	120

Angol rostélyos	Engl. Rostbraten	80
hizl. marhahusb.	von bestem Mastfleisch	80
Sült sódar tojással	Ham and eggs	
Tojáslepény	Omelette	
pusztán	naturelle	
gyümölcscsel	mit Früchten	
befőttel	aux Confiture	
felpuffantva	Soufflée	
fines herbes	fines herbes	
halikrával	mit Caviar	
gombával	Champignon	

Tojás-étkek. — Eierspeisen.

Kavart tojás	Gerührte Eier
Tojás-rántotta ajókával	Eierspeise mit Sardellen
2 drb tojás pörköltlében	2 Stück Eier in Pörköltsaft
2 " tojás tormával	2 " Eier mit Kren
Tojáslepény sódarral	Omelette mit Schinken

Menu, 1939

Kárpátia restaurant, 1995

"Székely goulash is not only a popular and truly delicious dish, it is also noteworthy for a number of reasons. In the first place, in reality it is not of Székely origin, it is unknown in Transylvanian peasant cooking. Secondly, not only the first part of its name, but the second too is misleading: it is not goulash. It does not belong to the goulash family: it quite obviously does not even resemble goulash – what is cabbage doing in a goulash? What then, is the origin of the name which, in Pest usage, has been transformed to Székely cabbage, quite logically, recalling Transylvanian cabbage dishes.

This is its third and greatest peculiarity.

The »godfather« of Székely cabbage was none other personality than Sándor Petőfi, and it was created by Petőfi's contemporary, József Székely, county chief archivist. The Komló Garden, where they were both regular customers, was located next door to the County Hall in what was then Gránátos Street (today: Városház Street). One day, in 1846, when Székely arrived late for lunch there was hardly any food left, and the choice was very limited. At the request of the guest, the willing innkeeper served what was left of the sauerkraut in sauce and the pork pörkölt together on the same plate. The improvisation proved to be tasty, with a pleasing flavour. Petőfi witnessed this, and next time he ordered the same dish for himself, tagging the name Székely to it. »Székely goulash« soon took root and became widely known. Later the sour cream was added, as both decoration and flavouring. We have to admit that it was an improvement..."

Elek Magyar: The Gourmet's Cookbook

Kárpátia restaurant, 1995

1898

Established: 1877

VI. *Nyugati tér*

Nyugati pályaudvar étterme

MCDONALD'S

The Eiffel firm of Paris designed the splendid Western Railway Station building and, of course, its restaurant too. The restaurant, opened in 1877, was owned by the railway company which invited tenders for its lease, from recognised specialists only. Thanks to this condition, the railway station restaurant became one of the most elegant restaurants in Budapest.

From 1896 Ernő Schuszter rented the premises and attracted clients with fresh draught Kőbánya beer, fine Hungarian wines, French and Hungarian dishes. In 1925 János Démusz who had already earned a reputation as the manager of the Győr railway restaurant, took over from Schuszter.

Although part of the fine furnishings survived, after the war the Nyugati was no longer regarded elegant, and did not have a particularly good cuisine either. Privatisation brought a new style to the old building: McDonald's opened one of its Budapest restaurants here. It is one of the most attractive units in the fast food chain's international network and it soon became popular with young people.

1934

Menu, 1933

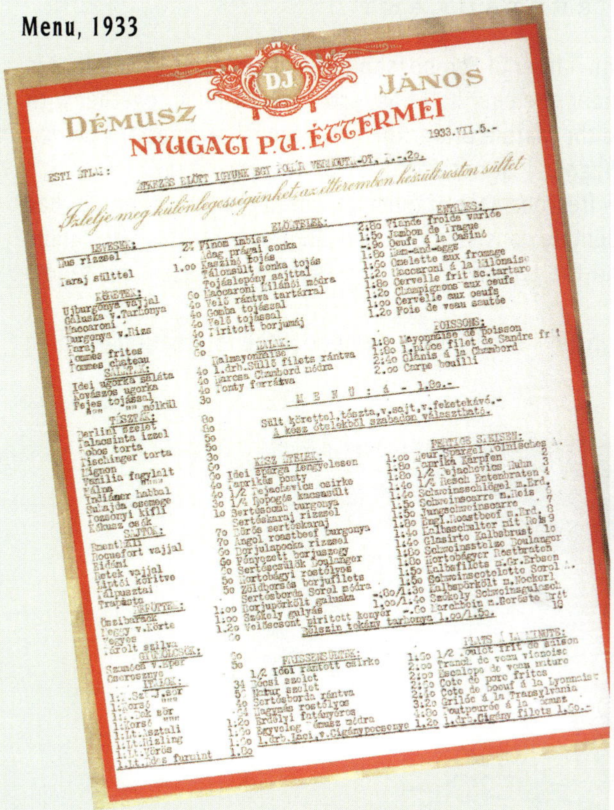

DÉMUSZ JÁNOS
NYUGATI P.U. ÉTTERMEI

1933.VII.5.-

ESTI ÉTLAP:

ÉTKEZÉS ELŐTT IGYUNK EGY POHÁR VERMOUTH-OT

Ízlelje meg különlegességeinket, az étteremben készült roston sültet

LEVESEK:
Lus rizzsel
Taraj sülttel

KÖRETEK:
Ujburgonya vajjal
Galuska v.Tarhonya
Maccaroni
Burgonya v.Rizs
Taraj
Pommes frites
Pommes chateau

SALÁTÁK:
Idei ugorka saláta
Kovászos ugorka
Fejes tojással
" " nélkül

TÉSZTÁK:
Berlini szelet
Palacsinta izzel
Tobos torta
Dischinger torta
Mignon
Vanilia fagylalt
Málna
Indiáner habbal
Sulajda csemege
Pozsonyi kifli
Kókusz csók

SAJTOK:
Ementhali
Rocquefort vajjal
Edámi
Petek vajjal
Liptói körítve
Pálpusztai
Trapista

BEFŐTTEK:
Őszibarack
Meggy v.Körte
Vegyes
Törölt szilva

GYÜMÖLCSÖK:
Szamóca v.Eper
Cseresznye

ITALOK:
1:Sör
1:Korsó
1:Dok sör
1:Korsó
1:Lt.Asztali
1:Lt.Rizling
1:Lt.Vörös
1.Lt.Édes furmint 1.60

ELŐÉTELEK:
2.4 Finom imbisz
Adag prágai sonka
1.00 Kasziné tojás
Tálonsült sonka tojás
Tojáslepény sajttal
60 Maccaroni Milánói módra
40 Velő rántva tartárral
40 Gomba tojással
40 Velő tojással
40 Piritott borjumáj
60
60

HALAK:
Halmayonnaise
40 1.drb.Süllő filets rántva
40 Barossa Chambord módra
40 Ponty forrázva
30

M E N Ü : á - 1.60.-

Sült körettel, tészta, v.sajt, v.feketekávé.-
A kész ételekből szabadon választható.

KÉSZ ÉTELEK:
60 Idei spárga lengyelesen
60 Paprikás ponty
40 1/2 Pejachevics csirke
40 1/4 Ropogós kacsasült
30 Sertéscomb burgonya
10 Sertéskaraj rizzsel
Sertéskaraj
70 Rörös sertéskaraj
70 Angol roastbeef burgonya
60 Borjulapocka rizzsel
60 Fényezett borjuszegy
60 Sertéscsülök Boulanger
50 Hortobágyi rostélyos
50 Zöldborsós borjufilets
Sertésborda Sorol módra
1:00 Borjupörkölt galuska
1:00 Székely gulyás
1.20 Velőscsont piritott kenyér
Bélszin tokány tarhonya 1.00/1.50.

FRISSENSÜLTEK:
1/2 Idei rántott csirke
34 Bécsi szelet
50 Natur szelet
40 Sertésborda rántva
Hagymás rostélyos
1:20 Erdélyi fatányéros
1:30 Vegyes ...módra
1:60 1.drb.Laci,v.Cigánypecsenye 1.20

ENTRÉES:
2:80 Viande froide variée
1:50 Jambon de Prague
-.90 Oeufs à la Casiné
1:80 Ham-and-eggs
1:60 Omelette aux fromage
1:20 Maccaroni à la Milonaise
1:80 Cervelle frit Sc.tartaro
1:20 Champignons aux oeufs
1:00 Cervelle aux oeufs
1.20 Foie de veau sautée

POISSONS:
1:80 Mayonnaise de poisson
1:80 1.pièce filet de Sandre frit
2:40 Glánis à la Chambord
2.00 Carpe bouilli

FERTIGE SPEISEN:
1:00 Heur.Spargel Polnisches A. 1
1:80 Paprika Karpfen 2
1:80 1/2 Pejachevics Huhn 3
1:40 1/4 Resch Entenbraten 4
1:40 Schweinsschlögel m.Erd. 5
1:50 Schweinscarre m.Reis 6
1:50 Jungschweinscarre 7
1:80 Engl.Roastbeef m.Erd. 8
1:40 Kalbsschulter mit Reis 9
1:40 Glasirte Kalbsbrust 10
1:80 Schweinsstelze Boulanger
1:80 Hortobágyer Rostbraten
1:50 Kalbsfilets m.Gr.Erbsen
1:60 Schweinscotelette Sorol A.
-.80/1:30 Kalbspörkölt m.Nockerl
1.00/1:40 Székely Schweinsgulasch
-.60 Herzbein m.Geröste Brot 18

PLATS À LA MINUTE:
1.60 1/2 Poulet frit de saison
2.00 Tranch de veau viennoise
2.00 Escalope de veau nature
2:60 Cote de porc frites
2:40 Cote de boeuf à la Lyonnaise
3.20 Grilée à la Transylvania
4:80 Poutpourée à la ...
1.drb.Cigány filets 1.60.-

McDonald's restaurant, 1995

Around 1900

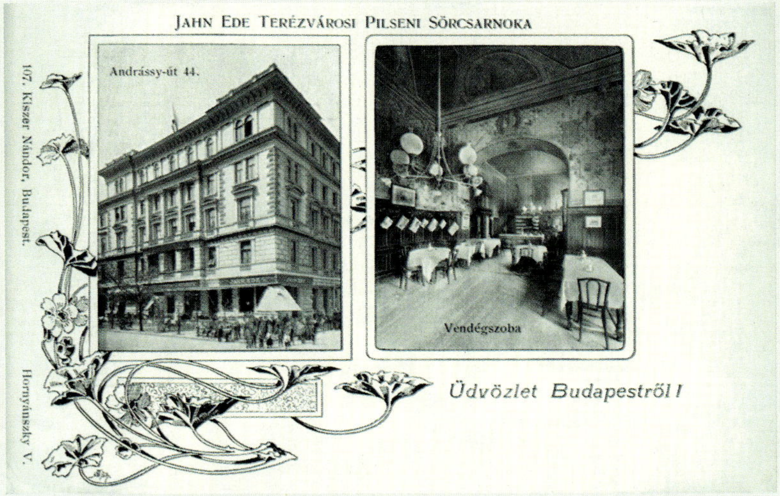

Established: 1885

VI. Andrássy út 44

Terézváros Pilseni Sörcsarnok

BOMBAY PALACE RESTAURANT

The Terézváros Pilsen Beer Hall was opened in 1885 by Ede Jahn, father of Ferenc Jahn who later became known for his activity in the workers' movement. After the death of the founder, the beer hall was taken over in 1904, together with János Rieber, by the Vilmos Wagner who had previously owned the Marble Bride. The new owners' calculations proved to be right: the establishment, popularly known only as the Wagner, lost nothing of its popularity.

In 1933 it was converted into a glittering bistro embellished by frescoes. One of them portrayed the composer who had the same name as the owner: Richard Wagner. The regular clientele consisted of musicians, singers, stage designers and ballet dancers from the neighbouring Opera House, and the famous guests - as well as the excellent food - attracted the prosperous middle-class too.

After nationalisation it was renamed Opera Restaurant, then in 1994 it became a member of the international Indian restaurant chain, the Bombay Palace.

1898

Bombay Palace restaurant, 1995

Menu
from the 1890s

JAHN EDE
TEREZVÁROSI PILZENI SÖRCSARNOK
BUDAPEST.
ANDRÁSSY-ÚT és GYÁR-UTCZA SARKÁN

REGGELI ÉTLAP * FRÜHSTÜCK-KARTE

kr.

Káposztaleves
Gulyásleves
Marha-gulyás
Szalon-tüdő czitrommal
Borjupörkölt
Tányérhus

Krautsuppe
Gulyás-Suppe
Rinds-Gulyás
Salon-Beuschel mit Citrone
Kalbs-pörkölt
Tellerfleisch

12
12
14
14
18
26

Bombay Palace
restaurant, 1995

Established: 1896 XIV. *Állatkerti út* 2

Wampetics vendéglő

GUNDEL ÉTTEREM

The building in City Park housing what is today perhaps Budapest's most prestigious restaurant, was erected in 1896 according to the plans of Ervin Bauer. Ferenc Wampetics, who leased the neighbouring Zoo Restaurant, had it built at his own expense in the pleasant green setting.

The Wampetics soon became famous for its tables under the shady trees, its elegant rooms and excellent cuisine and was made even more famous by its illustrious guests. Painters such as István Csók and Rippl-Rónai, various sculptors, politicians, poets, writers and popular actors such as Gyula Csortos and Ede Ujházi were regulars here. It was in honour of Ujházi that the dish still known as Ujházi soup was created in the Wampetics kitchen; its essential ingredients are chicken, a variety of vegetables and vermicelli.

In 1911 the lease of the restaurant was taken over by Károly Gundel who was later to become an outstanding Hungarian restaurateur. Although he was still only 27 at the time he had already gained experience in leading establishments in France, England, Switzerland and Germany. Writers, poets and journalists sang the praises of the dishes he created; Gundel pancakes, for example, assume a place in literature. Art and gastronomy met here in another way too. Károly Gundel's son Imre Gundel writes in his book "Memoirs of Catering" that guests seated at the tables outdoors could enjoy the excellent opera performances on the open-air stage of the zoo.

The Gundel family ran the business until it was nationalised, and subsequently Károly Gundel's sons worked there as employees. During privatisation it was purchased by Roland Lauder and a famous Hungarian gastronomer from the USA, George Lang. In 1992 they restored the splendid restaurant to its original style. George Lang personally ensures the highest standards.

1917

Az első magyar részvény serfőződéből
1 pohár sör 30.—

A. 1922 X 12. dében

RESTAURANT GUNDEL ÉTTERMEI

GRAND HOTEL
ROYAL
NAGYSZÁLLODA
BUDAPEST,
VII. ERZSÉBET-KÖRÚT 45-47
TELEFON: JÓZS. 119-27.

NYÁRON:
ÁLLATKERTI
KÜLSŐ VENDÉGLŐ
EN ÉTÉ
PRÈS DU JARDIN
ZOOLOGIQUE
VI. VÁROSLIGET
TELEFON: 24-43.

A FÉNYŰZÉSI ADÓ AZ ÁRAKBAN BENNFOGLALTATIK.

Hors d'Oeuvre

1 személyes vegyes izelitő à 400.—
Oeuf farci.
Chaudfroid de Volaille.
Mousse de foie gras.
Mayonnaise de Poisson
Salade de Boeuf
Sardine.
Salami — Beurre
400.— Kor. Par personne

Leveseк Potages Suppen

Finom meteit 11.—
Szárnyas ragout 40.—

Napi főzelék

Sav. káposza feltéttel 45.—

Marhahus

Paradicsom mártás és burg 330,—

Köretek — Légumes — Gemüse

Zöldbab — Tök Paraj 40.—
Pár. káp. 40 Tarhonya 40 Maccaroni 40.—
Rizs — 50. Haricots vert à l' Anglaise 120.—
Petits pois a l' Anglaise 120.—
Choux brüxelles à l' Anglaise 120.—
BURGONYA — POMMES de TERRE
Sós 30 — Resztelt 40.—
Pom. chateau 70.— Pommes sautées 80.—
Pommes frites 140.—

Saláták Salades Salate

Paradicsom — Ugorka 50.—
Paprika — Cékla — Burgonya 40
Kovászos ugorka — Fejessaláta 40.—
Fejes tojással 70.— Vegyes 60.—

Befőttek — Compotes — Dunstobst

Párolt Alma Körte 90.—
Cseresznye Meggy, Dinnye 150.—
Ringló Szilva Őszi és Sárgabarack 150.—
Vegyes befőtt 180.—
Californiai barack 250.—

Sajtok — Fromages — Käse

Ementhali 90.—
Trappista Pusztadóri — Óvári 40.—
Pál-pusztai 44.—

Gyümölcs — Fruits — Obst

adag Szőllő 80.— adag Dió 50.—
Őszi barack — Alma — Körte ?
Vegyes gyümölcs 120.—

Tészták — Entremets — Mehlspeisen

Tojásos galuska 80.—
Szőllős és Almás rétes 90.—
Valeria torta 80.—
Caramel crém 100.—
Gesztenye pürré tejszinhabbal 100.—

Étkezés előtt igyunk 1 pohár GUNDEL-COCKTAILT 100

Hideg előételek — Entrées Froides

1 töltött tojás Record módra 120 — 1 oeuf farci à la Record
Szárnyas saláta olasz módra 250.— Salade à l'Italiènne
Oroszhus saláta 250.— Salade de boeuf à la Russe
Kocsonyázott libamáj 200.— Mousse de foie gras
Kocsonyázott szárnyas hus 250.— Chaudfroid de volaille
Attört sonka kocsonyában 200.— Medallion de jambon
1/2 Jérce 500.— 1/2 Poularde
adag Liba 580.— Oison roti
Straszburgi LIBAMÁJ PÁSTÉTOM 600.—
Angol bélszin tartár márt. 475.— Filet de boeuf sce tartar
Sonka aspic-kal 250.— Jambon aspic
Szalámi 120 Salami
1 drb szardinia 70 — 1 Sardine

Halak — Poissons

KOCSONYAZOTT PONTY 450.— CARPE en GELÉE
Hal mayonnaise 300.— Mayonnaise de Poisson
Fogas froid sauce Remoulade 600.—
Balatoni süllő roston ? ? Sandre du Balaton grillée
Balstoni fogas Normand módra 650.— Fogas du Balaton à la Normand
Harcsa Meuniere m. 600.— Glanis à la Meuniere
Ponty rántva 450 — Carpe frit

Meleg előételek — Entrées chauds

Tojáslepény sajttal 255 — Omelette au fromage
Tojás serpenyőben hercegnő m. 255.— Oeufs en cocotte à la Reine
Lágy tojás Valentin m. 255.— Oeufs poches à la Valentienne
Habart tojás zöld borsóval 255.— Oeufs brouille au petits pois
Gomba tojással 200.— Champignons aux oeufs
Velő tojassal 250.— Cervelle aux oeufs
Kelvirág vajas morzsa 200.— Choux-fleur Polonaise
Csirag Lengyel m 360. Asperges à la Polonaise

Kész ételek — Plats du Jour

1/2 Jérce 500. 1/2 Poularde
adag Liba 580.— Oison roti
adag Pulyka 450.— Dindonneau roti
Pörkölt ponty galuskával 400. — Carpe à la Hongroise
Angol bélszin burg. 475 Filet de boeuf à l' Anglaise
Borju vesés parajjal 315.— Longe de veau au épinards
Paradicsomos borju comb rizs 315 — Cuisse de veau en tomate
Tejfeles borju szelet macc. 340.— Escalope de veau a la crème
Sertés karaj pár. káposzta 320.— Carre de porc choucroute
Elszászi sertés borda 320 — Cotelette de porc à la Alsacienne
Töltött rostélyos burg. 460.— Cote de boeuf farcie
Csíkos tokány rizi-bizi 225.—

Frissen készült ételek — Plats à la Minute

Tournedos Medicis 640.—
Rumpsteak grille à la Moelle 560
1/2 Piritott Csirke gombával 500 — 1/2 Poulet sautée aux champignons
1/2 rántott csirke 420.— 1/2 Poulet panné
Libamáj szeletkék Perigoram m. 600.— Filet de foie gras pannée sce Perigoram
Bélszin filet Carmen m 560.— Filet Mignon Carmen
Borju borda Bécsi m. 430.— Cotelette de veau à la Vienoise
Hizott rostélyos hagymával 560 — Cote de boeuf primée à la Lyonnaise
Borjusteak serpenyőben 450.— Steak de veau en casserolle
Piritott borjumáj rizs 300.— Foie de veau sautée Lyonnaise
Csirkemáj risotto 300.— Risotto foie de volaille
Chateau briand primeé ?

KLÓSZ GY. ÉS FIA BUDAPEST

Menu, 1922

Early 1910s

"... *Squabbling is almost unavoidable when crab soup is being cooked, because it imposes more work on the kitchen staff than perhaps any other soup in the world...*

Szindbád continued what he had to say:

–... Work with them begins when they are still resting in the crab-basket and they have to be sorted, making separate piles for the tiny ones, known as Tisza crabs... The bigger ones, known as »Solo crabs« (Zala crabs)... It is from these larger crabs that the soup is actually made, while the tiny crabs serve simply as an addition.

– Let's not go too fast, interrupted the Gentleman. How did they cook the crabs?

– In beef stock, of course... The protesting crab is washed before it can take its place in the briskly boiling meat soup.

– It is sent live to the death of a martyr? – the Gentleman asked, staring incredulously.

–... Personally, I like crabs that go live and flapping into the boiling pot... The hot meat stock finishes the crab off in a minute anyway and then at ease it waits in the pot for the salt, caraway seed, parsley and the rest... By the time it comes out of here, especially the tinier kind, it is so docile it can be made to do anything. You can tear off its tail and pincers. Remove the green and black parts, the bitter ones from the shell and replace them with a filling of rice flavoured with parsley and egg. Only the yellow parts must be left in the shell. Then the crab goes back into the strained stock and can be left to continue cooking, until it is served..."

Gyula Krúdy: May Miracles

... "János Gundel (restaurateur to Jókai and Mikszáth) put his children to work in the kitchen at the age of six so that he could watch and observe their instinctive gestures to see who had a feeling for this special occupation which creates an art from meat, ginger, saffron, peppers, fish and sheets of pasta, the tiny head of cloves and fiery slivers of cherry peppers. His choice fell on his son Károly... who later made this kitchen world famous, publishing his one hundred and twenty recipes... in German, English, French and Czech... »who raised generations of waiters, chefs and confectioners...«

... Although he earned a fortune as the restaurateur of the former Wampetics, the City Park, and Hotel Gellért, he remained loyal to his homeland and in answer to the lucrative offer he received from the director of the London Ritz all he said was: »I shall stay here«..."

Péter Ruffy: The Gundel Family

Menu, 1995
Gundel restaurant, 1995

Established: 1902 *V. Kígyó utca 4-6*

Apostolok söröző

APOSTOLOK ÉTTEREM

In 1910 the only place in Hungary with Löwenbrau beer on tap was the Apostles. The bistro was established in 1902 by János Förster, a member of the second generation of a dynasty of restaurateurs. The successful business, at first known only as a taproom, was altered in 1913. The richly decorated interiors, partly divided into alcoves, were fitted with artistically carved furniture.

The enamel mosaics portraying the twelve apostles were not added and installed in their present place until the reconstruction and expansion carried out in 1929. Two years earlier the management had passed from János Förster to his sons, Pál and Miklós and by then Löwenbrau had gone from the drinks list which included Salvator and Dreher beers instead, as well as white, red and dessert wines, champagnes, liqueurs and mineral waters. This menu also featured the rules of the house, which called for "silence and sobriety".
This atmosphere still characterises the Apostles.

1906

1923

Container
for sausages, 1910

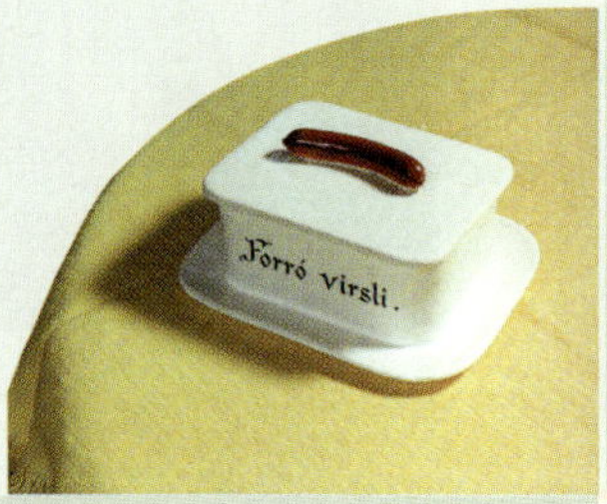

Menu, 1931

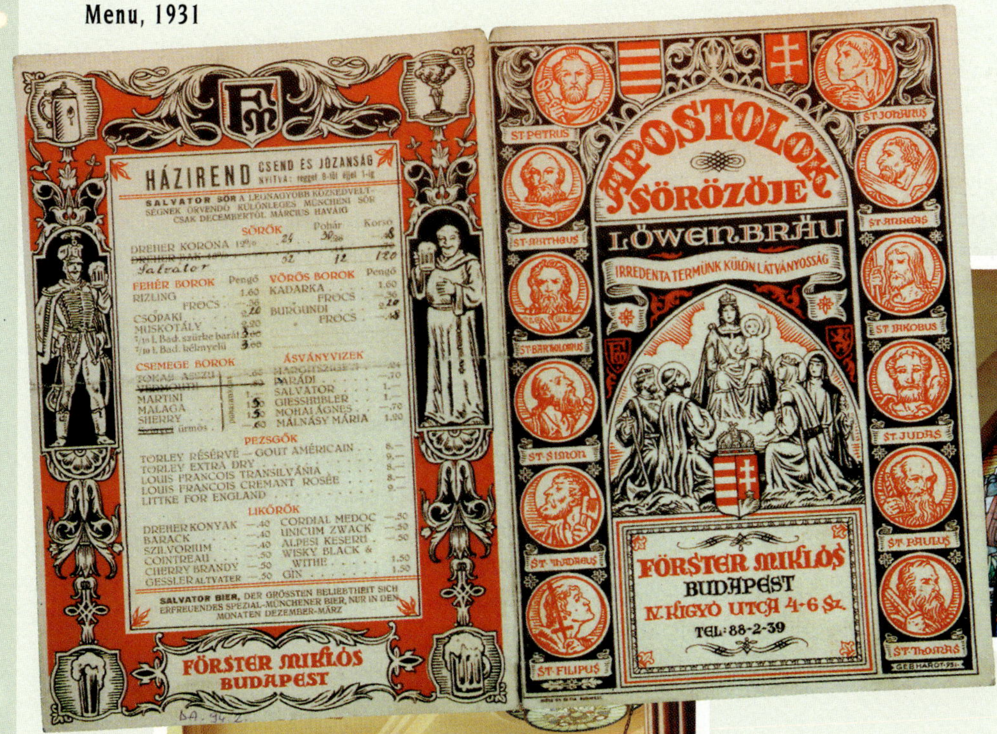

Apostolok restaurant, 1995

"The poet is sitting at a table with a red cloth in the Kiss Palcsi inn, although with his ruddy cheeks, jet-black beard and enormous appetite he seems more like a steward from the Pallavicini estate on a brief visit to the town. He eats a supper of fried fish and curd cheese strudel flavoured with dill, drinks light rosé wine, washes it down with black coffee, puffs Virginia tobacco afterwards, then nods in a friendly way in the direction of the counter:
– My bill, Uncle Palcsi!
– Aye, Mr. Pósa.
And when Uncle Palcsi adds up the fish, noodles, rosé, white bread, black coffee and black Virginia, which all comes to no less than thirty krajcárs, Lajos Pósa produces his latest volume of poetry from his pocket and places it on the table in front of Uncle Pali who, in a perfectly serious business transaction, counts out seventy krajcárs in change because it is clearly printed on the attractive cover of the book that its price is one forint."

Ferenc Molnár: The Poet

Established: 1904

V. *Március* 15. *tér* 7

Mátyás Pince étterem

In the early years of the century the Dreher Brewery had an apartment house built in the heart of the Inner City and, not surprisingly, it had a beer tavern installed on the ground floor. The brasserie was opened in 1904 under the management of Mátyás Baldauf (Borostyánkői) who already had experience in running a tavern. Business boomed; it attracted magnates, industrialists dropped in for a beer, artists formed table societies; several hectolitres of fresh draught beer were sold daily. Within just a quarter of a century – up to 1929 – the restaurant had to be expanded three times. At first it sold only cold snacks to go with the beer, but later hot dishes were also served.

Following reconstruction in 1937 the Matthias Cellar acquired an appearance befitting its name and clientele; the frescoes that can still be seen today, the stained-glass windows portraying scenes from the life of King Matthias and the ornamentations designed by Jenő Haranghy were all done then. In the same year the owner died and the management was taken over by the widow and her sons. The interior and furniture which were heavily damaged during the war, were later restored and listed.

For over a quarter of a century the nationalised Matthias Cellar was directed by Endre Papp, the doyen of gastronomy who was unsurpassed in expertise. He entertained thousands of prominent Hungarian and foreign guests, serving them dishes he created himself. Matthias Cellar, which has numerous rooms, still attracts large numbers of foreign tourists.

1923

1904

MÁTYÁS PINCE

BALDAUF MÁTYÁS VENDÉGLŐS

BUDAPEST, IV, ESKÜ-TÉR 6. SZ.

JUBILEUMI ÉTLAP

az 1904. január 30-án

LEVES

REGGELI ÉTLAP

Főzelék

Tészták

Sajtok

Halak

Saláták

Készételek

Borok

Menu, 1904

1910s

Mátyás Pince restaurant, 1995

Established: 1912

VIII. *Rákóczi út* 29

Wurglits vendéglő

ORCHIDEA ÉTTEREM

Records of the time mention the restaurant opened in Rákóczi Road in 1912 simply as the restaurant of Vilmos Wurglits, and noted that it was a meeting place for people from Vas, Somogy and Zala counties. Why people from the counties around Lake Balaton gathered in this distant Budapest restaurant is a mystery, but it is a fact that the Wurglits had special rooms suitable for large groups and banquets. It also sold wine it had produced, and served a range of typical Hungarian dishes.

From 1928 the restaurant was taken over by Milos Kovácsevics who was succeeded in 1933 by Dénes Bíró. He altered the restaurant in 1937 by installing alcoves in part of the interior, and carved furniture, and by increasing the capacity to 400–500 places; after the war, in 1945, he had it rebuilt. Not long after, however, this restaurant too met the fate of nationalisation, and operated for close to half a century under the name of Bástya (Bastion). In 1993 it was christened the Orchidea Restaurant.

Advertisement, 1920s

Heading of a menu, 1937

1942

Orchidea restaurant, 1995

Established: 1930 III. *Lajos u.* 46

Sipos Halászkert

RÉGI SIPOS HALÁSZKERT

Károly Sipos opened his restaurant at 46 Lajos Street in 1930. Previously, from 1922 to 1929 he had run an establishment known as the Sipos Fishermenís Garden at 43 Belső Jászberényi Road, in Kőbánya, which had become famous for its speciality, boneless fish soup. At first, business was poor in Lajos utca, but Sipos spent heavily on advertisements and succeeded in building up the business. The Sipos family had their own, enormous wine cellar where they stored Kadarka wine from Csongrád.

In 1943 the owner of the restaurant was Ferenc Kugler.

From the mid-1970s the old buildings in Óbuda were demolished and in 1984 the Sipos met this fate too. When the old district was rebuilt, in summer 1995 the old-new Sipos once again opened in Lajos Street.

1930s

Signboard, 1995

Poster, 1922

"People who like fish and, given the opportunity, place it above all other dishes, say that it is possible to distinguish, right from the first spoonful of liquid, between lake fish, Danube and Tisza fish. Old fishermen will insist that fish should never be cooked in any other water than the water of the Tisza. Other water is just no good. When fish is cooked in other water, it cannot be said that habet colorem, odorem et saporem. Neither its colour, nor its flavour, nor its odour will be what it should be. In addition, »decent people« use no other implement than a spoon to eat paprikás fish. Anyone who takes up a knife and fork does not deserve this princely dish."

István Tömörkény:
Here we go, cooking again

Régi Sipos restaurant, 1995

Plate for fishbones, 1900

"The Lord knows: I am not very fond of coffee, but after all, one dislikes tax but pays it nevertheless. I regard the price of coffee rather as an entry fee to the coffee-house where I find great enjoyment: a little newspaper, a little gossip, looking on quietly at the chess and card-table, friendly handshakes, different faces and ways of speaking, virtuosity at billiards – all of them very pleasing pastimes... This is life in the coffee-house, one enjoys himself and at the same time he is annoyed at those 15 krajcárs. One could not wish for more for that sum."

Géza Gárdonyi: Diary

Established: 1832 — V. *Vigadó tér* 2

Vigadó kávéház

VIGADÓ ÉTTEREM ÉS SÖRÖZŐ

The old Redoute (Vigadó), the scene of concerts and balls, was opened in Vigadó tér in 1832 in the centre of the Inner City's entertainment district. The Vigadó coffee-house was located on its ground floor. The building was designed by a leading architect, Mihály Pollack who divided the vast coffee-house interior with columns. From 1847 the leaseholder was the same Ferenc Privorszky who had earlier brought fame to the Pilvax coffee-house. His activity here did not last long because the Redoute was burnt down in 1849.

Then, in the 1850s, a hastily built inn known as the Redoute Glass Salon operated in the centre of Vigadó tér. The new Redoute was not completed until 1865. Ferenc Deák, the liberal statesman, recommended his own room waiter, Márk Hangl who leased the coffee-house together with the summer kiosk from 1870. The following year he opened the Café Park in the square; the people of Pest called it simply the Hangli. It was a highly popular place; it offered strong coffee with half the usual quantity of water, cold snacks and a wide selection of cakes. It did not lose its clientele even when it was the Hangli in popular name only. After Márk Hangl, from 1888 to 1890 the leaseholder was Róbert Rémi jr. Around that time the establishment began to decline.

Lajos Evva, theatre director and writer, took over the lease in 1906 and made the coffee-house a flourishing business again. He was followed in 1933 by the Rónai brothers who transformed the coffee-house into a Hungarian-style bistro and the kiosk into a modern café-restaurant.

The Redoute building was destroyed again during the war and after long construction work it opened in 1980 with the present Vigadó restaurant on its ground floor.

1889

Leaflet from the 1920s

1837

1905

KAFFEEHÄUSER

COFFEE-HOUSES

"The Budapest public still frequents the »Hangli«, guests from the country arrange to meet in the »Hangli«, and foreigners are also sent to the »Hangli«. Because almost everyone turns up there...

... And what is the reason for this pilgrimage to the coffee and icecreams of the »Hangli«? Undoubtedly, at first it was the beautiful view that attracted people, the Danube, Chain Bridge, the hills across the river, the fresh air...

... But now, even if a curtain were lowered to block out the view of Buda, people would still flock here, simply because it is now in the vogue. The latest achievements of ladies' and gentlemen's fashion, the most beautiful hats and gowns, fascinatingly low-cut shoes, the bright diamonds and various other »little nothings« are sported there, and, of course, also the charming faces that peep out from under those »charming« hats. The fact that people also take coffee and icecreams here is of secondary importance. The two main things are: to see and to be seen..."

Kiosk beside the Danube. Fővárosi Lapok, 1889

1903

Vigadó restaurant, 1995

1848

Established: 1838

V. Pilvax köz 3

Café Renaissance

PILVAX ÉTTEREM ÉS SÖRÖZŐ

Ferenc Privorszky, who was later leaseholder of the Vigadó Coffee-house, opened his business at today's 7 Petőfi Sándor Street in 1838. At the time this was probably the most up-to-date coffee hall in Pest; it was certainly the first to have gas lamps. Károly Pilvax, who owned the business in the Inner City from 1842 to 1846, gave the coffee-house a new name which his successor, János Fillinger, retained.

In 1848 the Pilvax Coffee-house entered Hungarian history. Even earlier it had been a meeting place for radical youth, but during the revolution it was here that Petőfi and his companions drafted their demands, the Twelve Points and it was here that the poet first recited the National Song. On 15 March the Pilvax was the headquarters of the leaders of the revolution.

After the defeat of the revolution, when the name of the street was not yet Petőfi Sándor but Herrengasse, the same name figured on the sign-board. It was only after 1870 that it was again called Pilvax, when Antal Schőja was the owner from 1867 to 1895. He was followed by János Schovanetz, who had been head waiter. The building housing the Pilvax was demolished in 1911 and an enormous palace was built on the site. Pilvax Way was created at that time and the coffee-house was, once again, opened here, with Schovanetz still the owner.

The present Pilvax Restaurant was opened after renovation in the late 1960s.

1848

"We enjoy great respect in Vienna! Every morning the camarilla sends to the chancellery to ask what Berci Pákh said in the Pillvax. What is more, the moment her majesty Sophie opens her eyes in the morning, she has someone ask Metternich whether or not that Petőfi has said something angry in the Pillvax."

Mór Jókai: Petőfi and other citizens of Pest-Buda

The Pilvax coffee-house at the turn of the century

Pilvax restaurant, 1995

"To the right in the dimly-lit depth of the coffee-house, near the corner, stood a large, square wooden table with 8-10 chairs. This table formed the centre of the historical gatherings in the Pilvax. The young generation of writers, in particular, had long been particularly fond of this spot...

More than one ideal, more than one reform proposal which later became reality in those lively times, was conceived here in the coffee-house, at this square table. Like the blood circulation from the heart, all patriotic movements started from here in those times. Very appropriately, it was called the »public opinion table«..."

György Gracza: History of the Hungarian War of Independence, 1849–49

Around 1894

Established: around 1842

I. Szarvas tér 1

Szarvas kávéház

ARANYSZARVAS VENDÉGLŐ

The house was built in the 18th century, and was rebuilt a year after the 1810 fire. A relief depicting a running stag chased by hounds decorates the façade and according to contemporary records this was where the name of the building came from, that of the coffee-house and later the square. The "Zum Hirschen" coffee-house first appeared on this spot in 1842. The business was located in the corner of the building jutting into the square and had a coloured glass veranda. Around 1860 it was run by Elek Martinovics.

According to records dating from 1869 the Stag also operated for a while as an inn. The establishment was owned in 1864 by János Latner, in 1912 by Rezső Hoyer, then in the 1930s István Persl ran the coffee-house.

The business was nationalised after the war and since the 1960s it has operated as a game restaurant.

1910s

"Budapest now has more than one million inhabitants. If we deduct the upper ten thousand from this enormous figure, we are still left with at least a million citizens who rarely go to the theatre, a locale or cinema, and are content if they can occasionally sit at a marble table in a coffee-house, or can have a lunch or supper in a restaurant.

It is real entertainment, or at least a pastime, if Mr. Kovács can afford the luxury of a coffee-house breakfast on Sundays:

– Bring me a full breakfast, waiter, and the morning papers!

The term »full« is of recent use; it used to be called »Viennese breakfast«. Just like the full version, the Viennese breakfast comprises coffee, chocolate or tea and with it, as a delicious accompaniment, go butter, ham, jam, honey, perhaps a little tasty salami or sardines."

István Bródy: Entertainment in today's Pest

Aranyszarvas restaurant, 1995

Around 1910

Established: 1871

V. Vigadó tér 3

Szidon kávéház

DUNACORSO ÉTTEREM

For almost 40 years the coffee-house was known as the Szidon, then in the early 1910s, when Lőrinc Ulits took over the business for a short time, it was called the Ulits Coffee-house. Later it was renamed Dunacorso café-restaurant. Lajos Paulin, owner of the Negresco Coffee-house and the Prince of Wales Restaurant, who took over the Dunacorso in 1940, played an important role in the life of the establishment. The following year he carried out alterations, converting part of the coffee-house into the Ambassadeur luxury restaurant and bar where there was no dancing. Paulin's Dunacorso was a popular and prosperous business.

Nationalisation blurred its glitter for a relatively short time only. The Inner City Catering Enterprise placed its management in the hands of József Schuch, an exceptionally talented restaurateur and businessman, at first on a profit-sharing basis and later with a lease. Schuch served enormous portions, charged his impoverished regular guests symbolical sums and even in the most difficult times always had goose-liver, fresh, warm goose crackling and stuffed breast of veal on the menu. After his death, his widow and daughter took over the business.

Menu, 1943

Brochure
from the 1930s

1927

Dunacorso restaurant, 1995

"... Budapest has long been a famous coffee-house city, it was the »city of coffee-houses«.

In its six or seven hundred coffee-houses of all orders and ranks, big or small, rich or poor, noisy or quiet, decent or degenerate, but highly varied and individual, every citizen of the capital found his own table, black coffee or cappuccino tamed with milk and his friendly company; the lawyer his clients, the agent his market, the lottery-ticket seller, or vendor offering braces, pocket-knives or cuff-links his buyers, the poet his muse. The conscientious researcher studying the history and life of the citizens of Budapest will find in the history of our coffee-houses countless exciting data worth noting, and leading to conclusions. The citizenry of Budapest has, for the most part, lived, dreamed, watched and caroused the last hundred years in the coffee-house. Besides that, it has also worked there, and – although somewhat haphazardly and superficially – nurtured, cultivated and promoted commerce, industry, literature, the arts and the press..."

Jenő Heltai: The flowering and waning of the coffee-house

Established: 1875

VIII. *Múzeum krt.* 12

Schodl kávéház

MÚZEUM KÁVÉHÁZ ÉTTEREM

Baron Károly Fechtig had the house built in 1875 according to the plans of Antal Szkalnitzky. The ground floor was designed as a coffee-house. In the 1870s it operated as the Schodl Coffee-house. In the 1880s it was owned by the Engel family, and the business located next door to the National Museum was then known as the Museum Coffee-house. The regular clientele comprised university students, members from the house of representatives in Sándor Street, and writers. From 1909 the business was managed by József Gruber, then by his brother Károly, and from 1927 by Antal Frenreisz. From the 1930s the Museum Coffee-house flourished under the direction of Jenő Jovich who attracted the bohemian artistic world.

The elegant coffee-house, with new owners, experienced a renaissance in the early 1990s: it became a popular lunch and supper place mainly attracting entrepreneurs.

The tiles and tile pictures on the walls of the Museum Coffee-house were made in the Zsolnay factory in the 1880s and the fresco of a horseherds' race is the work of Károly Lotz. The surviving sections of the even earlier wooden panelling are also listed.

Coffee percolator from the turn of the century

Around 1910

Múzeum coffee-house restaurant, 1995

"He is the best in his trade in the world – and he falls on his feet wherever fate may take him. In Monte Carlo, just as in the railway restaurant at Pomáz. He is discreet, skilful, attentive – his mind is sharp, he understands a delicate situation in an instant, whether it is of a material or moral nature. He will not tell anyone who you were huddled together with confidentially the other day in the little alcove beside the window, and there is no need to draw his attention to this – he notices if you have forgotten your wallet at home, he wards off unpleasant strangers who want to sit at your table, and when he answers the telephone he can judge by the tone of voice whether you are there for someone or whether to say you are not.

There is something of Figaro in him and something of a déclassé Almaviva who bears his fate with humour.

It is not by chance that Hungarians address him as Főúr (Chief Gent).

*

He has been standing there beside the cash desk for half an hour and does not come near my table, although they are changing shift and he should be settling his accounts.

Perhaps he knows that I am writing about him.

He almost certainly knows, he knows everything, only he does not talk unnecessarily.

He has seen you, citizen of Pest, born and live in the coffee-house and if one day you drop dead in your chair, you could not wish for a more brotherly hand than his to close your eyes.

Frigyes Karinthy: The Pest waiter

EMKE coffe-house (on the right side), 1910

Established: 1894

VII. Erzsébet krt. 2

EMKE kávéház

CHICAGO BREWERY RESTAURANT

Jónás Wassermann, who earlier had a well known business in today's Deák Square, opened the coffee-house in 1894. Previously Mihály Wéber had an inn here. The name EMKE is the Hungarian abbreviation of the Transylvanian Hungarian Public Education Association in which Wassermann was an enthusiastic member. After his sudden death in 1901 the business was inherited by his son, Mór, who returned home from abroad and enriched the EMKE with many new ideas. Mór Wassermann began a programme of dynamic development. He created his own confectionery unit, installed a real bar which was something new in Hungary at the time, and he was the first to take the cabaret into the coffee-house as entertainment.

Like his father, he died young and in the 1930s the EMKE was taken over by Károly Horti and then József Berman. In 1937 the coffee-house was renovated and expanded, a grill added and a lift installed to take coats down to the cloakroom in the basement. The bandstand could be raised and lowered. In 1941 Géza Kövessy bought the business which suffered war damage in 1944. After nationalisation it was renovated, and it operated as a coffee-house until 1956. An espresso, a restaurant and a bistro, and later a hotel was opened in the building under the name of EMKE. Since renovation in 1988 the Chicago Brewery Restaurant has been operating on the site of the former coffee-house.

Mirror-covered wall with picture, 1910s

1910s

"Budapest is a city of table societies. There is perhaps no other city with such a highly-developed coffee-house and restaurant life as the Hungarian capital, and Budapest wits are right when they mention this characteristic of ours in the following way:

– Where do you live, sir?

– In the house which does not yet have a coffee-house.

The resident of Budapest is a slave to the marble and white table. The dearest sight to his eyes is the circle of cheerful faces around the coffee-house and restaurant table, and the sweetest music to his ears is the merry chatter, the laughter and tinkle of glasses that mingle with the smoke-filled air..."

Andor Gábor: Difficult inventory

"There was light and warmth in the coffee-house and entering it from the dim candlelight of our environment, we no longer felt so forlorn after all. Our friends were there, and all our refuge was there..."

Milán Füst

Chicago Brewery restaurant, 1995

Established: 1894

VII. *Erzsébet krt.* 9–11

New York kávéház

NEW YORK KÁVÉHÁZ ÉS ÉTTEREM

The New York insurance firm built an eclectic, yet magnificent palace on the Grand Boulevard in Pest, designed by the talented Hungarian architect, Alajos Hauszmann. In 1894 Europe's most sumptuous coffee-house, the New York, was opened on the lower floors. Only marble, bronze and other quality materials were used for the interior which was decorated with frescoes by leading painters including Károly Lotz, Gusztáv Mannheimer and Ferenc Eisenhut.

The first owner of the coffee-house was Vilmos Steuer, followed from 1900 by the Harsányi brothers. Under their management the New York became the number one literary coffee-house in Budapest. It was frequented by journalists from the editorial offices in the neighbourhood; in fact, the journalists, writers and poets who published many of their works in the papers, practically lived here. Famous actors, painters, musicians and sculptors added to the glamour of their table societies. This status was not changed after the coffee-house was purchased in 1913 by the Bánó and Szabó firm. Vilmos Tarján, the legendary journalist, newspaper editor, theatre director and leaseholder of numerous restaurants, rented the New York, too, from 1920. He established the restaurant and bar. It was during Tarján's time that the New York became a centre not only of literary but also of night life.

During the Great Depression, when Tarján declared bankruptcy in 1936, the New York was taken over first by Menyhért Kraszner, then a year later by Lajos Patat. The last leaseholder was Károly Spolarich in 1943. The building was damaged during the war, but a bistro, snack bar and bar were opened here in 1947 and closed two years later. In 1954 a restaurant was again opened, under the name of Hungária. The New York coffee-house did not regain its original name until the nineties.

Late 1890s

1894

1900

Around 1940

"But to return to the coffee-house, the wonderful thing is that everyone feels at ease there. The person who sits over an eighty-fillér black coffee all evening delighting in the women parading, as though in a fashion revue, and the person who helps himself to hors d'oeuvres from silver trays in the »deep water«. As though to prove this claim, the story of the bohemian's weekend was born in the New York:

Someone said that a certain bohemian usually spends the weekend in the New York.

– And what does he do? – he was asked.

– He comes in on Saturday evening, drinks a coffee and leaves the coffee-house on Monday morning. Oh yes, it must be added that this coffee-house is open day and night, without a break."

Photography in Pest: Café New York
Szinházi Élet (Theatre Life), 1927

Menu, 1929

"No one invited me here, I just dropped in once for breakfast and I stayed here, because they are right when they proclaim that a person must belong to a country, to a county, village, family, party, to be placed firmly somewhere in life. Well, a person must belong to a coffee-house too..."

Andor Gábor

New York coffee-house and restaurant, 1995

"It was a speciality of the New York that people from all walks of life could be found in it at the same time. »A king, a gypsy,» and in fact, when aristocrats were in the bar, at exactly the same time, true in different places, on the balcony or in the coffee-house, there were musicians, croupiers and hangers-on.

Many people complained about this too, but it was my opinion that the New York is to Budapest what the Café de la Paix is to Paris. Anyone can come in here. As my friend György Wolfner used to say: not just the sturgeon but also the carp, which are naturally far more numerous."

Vilmos Tarján: From (t.v.) to Tarján

"**A** *sweet vanilla aroma wafts up from the workshop. I have myself led in. I see ice-cream containers cooled with ammoniac, Limburg liver paté, pike-perch in aspic, electric beaters, the pale dough of Linzer cake under rolling-pins, the golden yellow filling of cream slices in giant copper bowls. The chocolate machine works with a buzz. Raw colonial cocoa is poured into it at the top, and drips out at the bottom, with butter, sweetened with sugar, splattering the confectioners' white aprons with its brown clay. Oh, if only in my childhood I had been locked up in such a chocolate prison for at least two weeks! They sweep out three quarters of a kilogramme of chocolate waste every day. Even the wall has chocolate on it. One could have licked everything here."*

Dezső Kosztolányi: Confectioner

Around 1920 (Vilmos Ruszwurm, far left)

Established: 1827

I. Szentháromság u. 7

Schwabl cukrászda

RUSZWURM CUKRÁSZDA

The Viennese Ferenc Schwabl opened his confectioner's shop on Castle Hill in Buda in 1827. He died three years later, and his widow married Lénárt Richter, court confectioner to the Palatine József. Richter ran the business from 1840 until his death in 1846. He commissioned the mahogany inlaid cherry-wood furniture which still decorates the Ruszwurm. In 1846 the business was managed by the widow, and then from 1847 to 1867 it operated under the direction of the apprentice confectioner, Antal Müller.

After Müller's death his widow, and later his son-in-law, Vilmos Ruszwurm became the owner of the business which up until then had always been inherited on the female side. Experts in the trade hold that the Hungarian Linzer cake which is still one of the specialties of the confectioner's shop, was created in the Ruszwurm. Ruszwurm's clients included aristocrats, army officers and high-ranking officials.

Following Ruszwurm's death, from 1922 the business was operated by his associate, right up until nationalisation in 1951. The intimate, Biedermeier confectioner's shop was renovated in 1960. Its furnishings, which are listed, are the most important confectionery interior in Hungary.

Around 1920

CUKRÁSZDÁK

"A short gentleman and an attractive young girl walk through the Castle early in the morning. They part in Holy Trinity Square. The short gentleman enters the Ministry of Finance. He is the Minister of Finance, Baron Frigyes Korányi. The young lady hurries on and enters the Ruszwurm confectioner's. She is the daughter of the Minister of Finance, Baroness Blanka Korányi, now an apprentice confectioner with the old Ruszwurm...

Day after day, from six in the morning till one o'clock, Baroness Blanka Korányi diligently makes minces, cakes and rolls in the vaulted workshop of the pastry shop in Buda. She stands before the long table in her white confectioner's gown, a confectioner's cap covering her blond hair, and brushes the delicious plaited milk-loafs, mignons and cream cakes with sugar icing...

The old Ruszwurm, who has been baking his tasty pastries in his famous shop in Buda for fifty-nine years, proudly watches his aristocratic apprentice. Many distinguished persons have visited this romantic little shop since 1827, when a certain Leonard Richter established the confectioner's shop. Queen Elizabeth often sat at the cherry-wood tables with »Miss Ferenczy«, and even Francis Joseph himself... and heaven only knows how many others. Now grey-haired ladies from Buda, and lovers from Pest while away the time at the tables.

There is more talk of love in this confectioner's shop than in all the English novels ..."

Nándor Szűcs – Jenő Komlós: Under the rooftops of Pest
An aristocratic apprentice confectioner

1930s

1995

Established: 1858 — V. Vörösmarty tér 7

Kugler cukrászda

GERBEAUD CUKRÁSZDA

In 1858 Henrik Kugler set up his confectioner's shop in today's Nádor Square, then in 1870 moved it to its present place, in neighbouring Vörösmarty Square where the Privorszky Coffee-house had previously operated. Kugler frequently visited Paris, bringing back many novelties, such as the mignon and other cakes filled with butter cream, which he introduduced in his pastry shop. The elegant interior and the many delicious pastries and cakes made it very popular in elegant circles too. It was often said in those days that everyone who counted took afternoon tea here.
The famous Swiss confectioner, Emil Gerbeaud became a partner in 1884, then in the following year bought up the whole business, expanded and renovated it. He lowered the prices, attracting even more customers. He introduced the French style of pastry with light cream cakes, invented cognac cherries, which later spread throughout the world, and chocolate dragées. He sold his bonbons in Hungary and abroad in fancy wooden boxes of his own design and exported his specialities to Europe, North and South America and even the Far East.
After Emil Gerbeaud's death in 1919, his widow and son-in-laws continued to operate the business, right up until nationalisation. The name was then changed to Vörösmarty Confectioner's Shop and only in 1984 did it regain its old name, Gerbeaud.

Advertisement from the 1910s

1910s

1896

Gerbeaud confectooner's shop, 1995

"... The Gerbeaud is not always a little pink cake with a frilly white skirt whose sole purpose in life is to fill in the time between the roast and the cheese; on this occasion the Gerbeaud is a confectioner's shop in Gizella Square, the most elegant public place in Budapest, where archduchesses and ordinary ladies take their tea from identical cups, with cream, or rum, dark or light, depending on whether they received good or bad upbringing back at home from their mothers..."

The secrets of the Gerbeaud
Pesti Futár, 1910

Bonbon box from the 1910s

Gerbeaud confectioner's shop, 1995

"The staple cakes of the pastry shops: cream cake, the »potato«, the Indian bun and the Rigó Jancsi... the extremely delicious flavours often have an interesting story, the Rigó Jancsi and the Indian bun for example. The former pays tribute to the memory of the elopement romance of the famous Hungarian Gypsy violinist and the French Countess of Chimay at the end of the last century... and the Indian bun is one of the first confectionery products to be filled with whipped cream.

... at the beginning of the last century (in 1834) Ferdinánd Pálfy, who lived in Vienna, rented the Theater an der Wien and had an Indian acrobat perform in an operetta. To popularise the production he had a renowned confectioner make the first Indian bun. Since then, devotees seeking out its various forms have even found specimens measuring 25 centimetres across."

Elek Magyar: The Gourmet's Cookbook

Bonbon box from the 1910s

1907

Established: 1870

II. *Fény utca* 8 / V. *Kossuth Lajos utca* 14–16

Auguszt cukrászda

Elek Auguszt, master confectioner, established his business in 1870 in the Tabán district, in house No. 654 that stood in what is now Dózsa Square. The shop became widely known after 1880 when it operated at 15 Attila Boulevard (today's 2 Attila Road). The founder's son, József Auguszt transferred the shop in 1902 to 10 Attila Boulevard (now 31 Attila Road). Five years later he opened an elegantly furnished business at 1 Krisztina Square with three rooms where afternoon tea was served, and workshops which also made chocolate, chocolate bonbons and dragées.

The Auguszt moved to 3 Krisztina Square in 1915. Here, the cakes were baked in steam ovens and the shop was resplendent with a Venetian mirror in a carved frame, a marble console table and a bronze clock.

The confectioner's shop in Krisztina tér, often called the Buda Gerbeaud, was destroyed in 1945. The founder's grandson, Elemér Auguszt, once again opened a pastry shop on the same site in 1947. After nationalisation, the prestigious Auguszt name was removed from the facade and since 1951 it has been called the Déryné Patisserie.

Today's Auguszt Confectioner's Shop was opened in 1957 in Fény utca by Mrs. Elemér Auguszt. This shop operates under the management of József Auguszt, the founder's great-grandson. In 1993 his sister, Olga Auguszt opened a branch shop in the 5th district, in Kossuth Lajos Street which is supplied with the delicious products from the confectionery workshop in Fény Street.

Bonbon box
from the 1910s

Auguszt confectioner's shop (V. Kossuth Lajos utca 14–16), 1995

"There are only two men, two small children and six women sitting in the main room of the confectioner's. Admirable fathers are having afternoon tea served to their sons who are plunged up to their elbows in the delights of cream cakes, chocolate doughnuts and cream rolls. The women lazily rest their elbows on the little marble tables. In front of them tea steams in silver pots. Without exception they all drink their tea without sugar. They meditate on their forty-six kilogrammes, the scales at the swimming pool and the ideal of beauty of the age. From time to time they take out their hand mirrors, powder their noses, redden their lips, then sip a little spoonful of bitter tonic, giving the observer the impression that they take their tea with rice powder and take occasional bites of a little stick of paint to go with it."

Dezső Kosztolányi: Confectioner

**Cup with spout
from the 1910s**

DUNAPALOTA
16

HOTELS

"Do you know the poetry of hotels?...

– I could talk a great deal about it. There are family hotels, where we feel at home more than in our own nest, and at the same time independent, without the stiffness of the family. There are charming, intimate, pleasant hotels. There are sad hotels, especially in the country, which resemble an out-of-tune piano and induce melancholy with their blind mirrors and damp bed linen; then there are disheartening, cursed, fatal hotels in which it is advisable to commit suicide on November evenings. There are cheerful hotels, where the taps giggle. There are stern, ceremonious, silent hotels, gossiping hotels, dissolute hotels, cheeky hotels, ostentatious, raucous, upstart hotels, reliable, calm, gentlemanly hotels with the noble rust of the past; light-hearted hotels, sluggish hotels, healthy hotels where sunshine streams even from the drains, and sick hotels, where the table is lame, the chair limps and the cupboard is on crutches, the couch is hectic and the pillows lie dying on the bed. In all, there are a great many kinds of hotels."

Dezső Kosztolányi: Kornél Esti

Established: 1871

V. Apáczai Csere János u. 4

Grand Hotel Hungaria

MARRIOTT HOTEL BUDAPEST

The first five-storey building in Pest was erected by the First Hungarian Hotel Company, in neo-renaissance style. The 250-bed hotel opened in 1871 was regarded as entirely up-to-date in every respect. 133 of its rooms overlooked the Danube and on the ground floor there was a function room, a restaurant, a coffee-house, smoking and writing rooms and shops. A conference office, hairdressing salon, postal and telegraph office were located on the mezzanine floor and there was a chapel on the fourth floor. In the area above the restaurant there was a ballroom two stories high. In the early 1890s a hydraulic lift was installed.

The hotel's first owner was Lipót Schalek. During the interwar years the hotel was directed by Ottó Marencich who was well known in the hotel industry throughout the world, and for a while held the post of president of the International Hotel Alliance.

The building was burnt down in 1945. In 1948 it was rebuilt from the neighbouring Bristol Hotel and was opened as Duna Hotel. This was demolished in the 1960s and in 1969 the Hotel Duna-Intercontinental, a five-star luxury hotel, was opened on the site.

In the course of privatisation in 1993 the hotel joined the Marriott hotel chain which renovated the rooms and altered the restaurants. The five-star hotel on the Danube, now in foreign ownership and under foreign management, applies the US Marriott standards in all respects. Today it is one of Budapest's top hotels.

1900

1910s

Menu cards

GRAND HÔTEL HUNGARIA
BUDAPEST

DISZEBÉD
AZ ÉJSZAKSARKI EXPEDITIO TAGJAI TISZTELETÉRE.
BANQUET
À L'HONNEUR DES NAVIGATEURS DU PÔLE ARCTIQUE.
MENU DU 20. OCTOBRE 1874.

POTAGE.	POTAGE.
Tyúkreszelt-leves.	
HORS D'OEUVRE.	HORS D'OEUVRE.
RELEVÉS.	RELEVÉS.
	Roastbeef à l'anglaise.
ENTRÉES.	ENTRÉES.
RÔTS.	RÔTS.
	Salade & Compote
ENTREMETS.	ENTREMETS.
	Pudding à l'Impériale
	Champagne

1908. JAN. 11.

Az estebéd sora.

BRISTOL-SZÁLLODA. JELSZÓ: Pukkadj meg!

PRO APPETITORIO:
Papramorgó és sör.

LEVES:
Csicseri Borsó.

HAL:
Balatoni fogas, párolt bolondgombával.
Magyar asztali keresztelетlen fehér.

DERÉK-FOGÁS:
Bélszin-szeletek vetreczével à la financière. (T. i. à la Székely, Bálint és Pirniczényi.)
Lengyeli Carbenet, bár Apponyi-termék, de nem fekete, hanem vörös.

SÜLT:
Kóser malacz-pecsenye, ropogós, à la reb. Menáchem.
Párolt fekete szilva, krumpli- és káposzta-saláta.
Louis François „Székely-pezsgő".

TÉSZTA:
Piritott darás-körülmetélt à la Lőwy Árpád.
Turós-rétes bioskei turóval.
Káposztás-rétes à la Sallustius.

SAJT:
Puszta-dóri à la Hungaria-Benes.
Liptai turó, körözteti Bartóky.
Retek à la Révai.

GYÜMÖLCS:
Ewa almája, Ádám csutkája nélkül.

FEKETE KÁVÉ:
Java-kávé Medve-czukorral.

Bristol Hotel, 1915

Terrace of the hotel's coffee-house, around 1910

Hungária and Bristol Hotels, 1908

"He was the shaman and confectioner of Hungarian songs. He could trumpet on his violin, as though he were playing for some wild Hajduk dance with ghostly figures surging around him in a teeth-gnashing rage or in a gentlemanly strut; he could penetrate with his violin strains into the depths of the heart-hives where the honey of love is the sweetest. He was a virtuoso...

Kóczé was one of the most celebrated violinists of his time: he often stayed up all night in places where no trace of the road could be seen when the foggy winter morning came...

Blinking, with the air of a guinea pig in a dinner jacket, Anti Kóczé played his tunes in the white room of the Hungária for the deer-legged fine ladies who set out from home for supper in their evening dresses, with the emblems of fashion, green waists, snaking eyebrows, Gábor Kiss hair-dos, they moved like leopards, their painted eyes like the raven's, their naked arms like branches of white lilac, the »hotvolé« of Pest and the perfume of the elegant circles of Europe floating in the air, mingling with fragments of French and English in the jargon of Budapest filling the white-walled, red-carpeted room like the humming of a mill..."

Gyula Krúdy: Anti Kóczé

Bedroom, early 1900s

Winter garden, 1934

"The Hungária share hotel or, to use its official name which can also be read on the banners floating from its gables, the »Grand Hotel Hungária« recently opened in our city.
Pest has been enriched with a fine building, and life in Pest with a new convenience... it has 133 windows overlooking the unrivalled beauty of the Danube Embankment... the beautifully situated royal palace... Gellért Hill and the citadel, and the summer residences half-hidden in the greenery of distant Széchenyi Hill...
... Our hotel is up to the »standard of the age« or, to use a fashionable phrase, »on top of the job« as regards its furnishings and comfort; apart from the Grand Hotel in Paris and Vienna, there is hardly another in Europe that could vie with ours..."

Lajos Takács: The Hungária Hotel in Pest

Marriott Hotel Budapest, 1995

Established: 1872 V. Károlyi Mihály u. 11–15

Erzsébet Királyné Szálloda

ERZSÉBET SZÁLLODA

Queen Elizabeth authorised the use of her name for the hotel, opened in 1872 together with a coffee-house. Its first owners were the Schmidt brothers, followed by Lajos Bereczky in 1896, then by Vince Mayer. In 1908 the establishment was leased by Imre Szabó who shortly after purchased the six-storey building next door and converted it into a hotel as well.

Szabó had a bistro built in the cellar. This was opened in 1927 as the János vitéz bistro. The walls were decorated with paintings by Béla Sándor illustrating Sándor Petőfi's poem "János vitéz" (The Valiant John).

The hotel was closed in 1976 and was not opened again until 1985, with 123 rooms and three-star classification. In today's János Cellar guests can admire the listed furniture and restored frescoes.

ERZSÉBET KIRÁLYNÉ-SZÁLLÓ
BUDAPEST, IV, EGYETEM-UTCA 5
TELEFON: (SZÁLLÓ) J. 322-77, (ÉTTEREM) J. 322-78

Elsőrangú családi szálló a Belváros központján. 100 szoba. Központi fűtés. Vízvezetékes mosdók. Lift. Fürdőszobák.
1 ágyas szoba 4·50-től 9 pengőig
2 " " 6·00-tól 12 "
Napi teljes pensio 9 pengőtől.
Éttermében a legjobb cigányzene. Elismert jó konyha. Saját termésű somlói borok. Az Erzsébet-pince szépen berendezett söröző. Revier-rendszer. Mérsékelt árak.
SZABÓ IMRE, tulajdonos.

Leaflet from the 1930s

Around 1910

Menus, 1934 and 1995

Restaurant, 1910s

HOTELS

Coffee-house, 1916

Bedroom, 1914

Erzsébet Hotel, 1995

HOTELS

Established: 1873

XIII. *Margaret Island*

Margitszigeti Nagyszálló

RAMADA GRAND HOTEL

The building designed by Miklós Ybl, the 162-room spa hotel, was built in 1873 in the natural park on Margaret Island in the Danube. The medicinal spring water was piped into the bathrooms and a medical office was set up for guests. Although in those days the island was only accessible by boat, the Grand Hotel Margaret Island was almost always full. János Arany, the great Hungarian poet and unsurpassed translator of Shakespeare spent the last six summers of his life here (1877–1882), and wrote odes to the beauty of Margaret Island.

The Grand Hotel was modernised in 1934, making it a match for the world's most comfortable and finest health hotels, and was renamed the Palatinus. It regained its original name later. The establishment was closed in 1985; using the plans made by Ybl in the last century, it was altered and reopened in 1987. Since then the 162-room, four-star hotel, linked by an underground passage to the Thermal Hotel Margaret Island, has been a member of the Ramada chain.

1915

HOTELS

1930s

Foyer, 1920s

"... I was in the fortunate situation that after my years as a journeyman, at the age of twenty-three, I was already fluent in English and French. So Mihály Gellér asked me to be at the service of the queen, as a room waiter, for the month and a half that she was to spend in the Grand Hotel...

In the mornings craftsmen from the Inner City visited the queen, offering their very beautiful and very costly masterpieces...

On one occasion they presented hats in the salon. The red signal lamp lit up and I went in to her...

– Look, you see the world through a man's eyes, after all, – said Queen Farida, looking at herself in the gilded mirror, a hat with a bow and bouquet on her head – kindly tell me, which hat should I buy?

– Your Majesty, – I replied, – I cannot tell you this way. Please try them all on!...

And she tried on the five hats, one after the other.

– I liked the third one best – I said.

– Then I shall buy that one! – said Farida, and signalled to her maid to pay for the hat.

... Such was the relationship between a queen and »Császár« (= emperor). By the way, on another occasion I told her that I too was an »Empereur«, which is what my name means in Hungarian, only I lack the wealth and the empire that goes with it... She smiled over it."

Recollections of Ferenc Császár, head waiter,
on the visit made by Queen Farida of Egypt in 1938

HOTELS

HOTELS

Ramada Grand Hotel, 1995

1905

HOTELS

Established: 1878

VII. *Rákóczi út* 90

Központi (Central) Szálloda

GRAND HOTEL HUNGARIA

The four-storey, 70 room Central Hotel was opened in 1890 in Baross Square, opposite the Eastern Railway Station. It had a restaurant, a coffee-house, lift and electric lighting. Its owner was György Höllrigl, and later János Sprung jr. (Next to it was the first inn in the vicinity of the Eastern Railway Station, the Debrecen Hotel, opened in 1878 with 12 rooms. According to contemporary records, horse-dealers from the nearby horse market came here to seek entertainment. In the 1930s the hotel's restaurant became famous for its low prices and its menu which – as someone wrote at the time – was as long as the highway.)

The 162-room Imperial Hotel, designed by Ármin Hegedűs and Artúr Sebestyén, was opened between the Central and the Debrecen Hotels in 1917. Right up till the early 1940s this establishment was owned by Lajos Keleti.

In 1918 when the Central Hotel passed into the ownership of the Sprung and Lingel families, a corridor was built to link the neighbouring buildings to it. From then until 1935 Lajos Keleti leased the Central and managed it together with his own hotel, the Imperial. In 1935 the two hotels were separated.

During the war the Central Hotel was burnt down, the Imperial was later nationalised and reopened as Szabadság (Freedom) Hotel. In the lengthy renovations carried out in the 1960s only the facade of the former Imperial was retained and a new, 406-bed hotel was erected on the site of the earlier three hotels, the Central, the Imperial and the Debrecen.

In 1983 the Szabadság Hotel was again closed and following alterations and expansion, was opened in 1985 as the 511-room, four-star Grand Hotel Hungaria.

1918

Imperial Hotel, 1930s

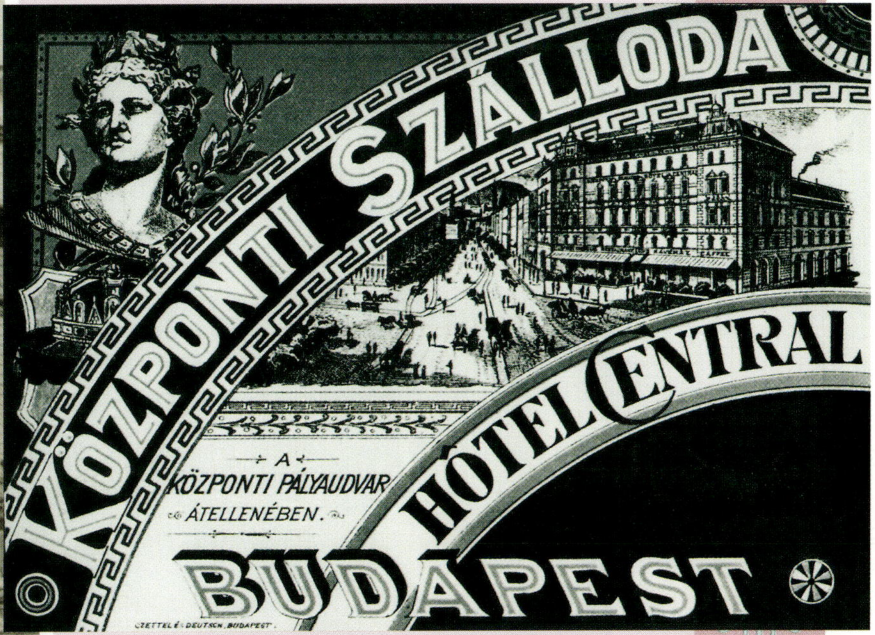

Advertisement from the 1920s

HOT

Grand Hotel Hungaria, 1995

Established: 1896 — VIII. *József krt.* 4

Rémi Szálloda

NEMZETI SZÁLLODA

The National Hotel owned by Róbert Rémi sr. once stood on what is now 9 Váci Street. He had the eclectic style hotel built on József Boulevard, using Zsolnay majolica for the interior decorations and curved Thonet wood panelling brought from Vienna. When it was opened in 1896, with a restaurant, coffee-house, wine tavern, winter garden, electric lighting, hot and cold running water and luxuriously appointed bathrooms, Rémi handed it over to his son-in-law, Vilmos Menyhért. From 1929 József Dénes was the hotel's owner and gave it the name of National Hotel.

The aged hotel was closed in 1986 and reopened in 1987, restored to the eclectic style of the turn of the century, with 76 rooms and three-star classification.

Nemzeti Hotel (centre), 1910s

1910s

1920s

Advertisements, 1896

Rémi szálloda

BUDAPEST.

Mély tisztelettel van szerencsém Czimedet a jelenkor minden igényeinek megfelelően épitett uj szállóm megtekintésére meghivni. A Rémi-szálló elsőrangu szálló a főváros kellő közepén, szemben a népszinházzal, a villamos és lóvasút által közvetlen összeköttetésben ugy a keleti mint a nyugoti pályaudvarokkal, nem különben a székes főváros minden egyes pontjával.

A szállóhoz nagyszabásu kávéházat és étkező termet rendeztem be, melyek mindegyike a maga nemében a legmagasabb szinvonalon áll. Gondoskodtam izlésesen berendezett salons particuliers-ről, valamint egy igen elegáns szabadon álló étkező terrászról. A szálló szobái nagy kényelemmel és fényűzéssel vannak berendezve, u. m. angol mosdó asztalokkal (állandóan meleg és hideg vizzel) villamos világitással, központi gőzfűtéssel stb. stb. A szállóban lift is van alkalmazva ugyszintén gondoskodva van fürdőszobákról is. A földszintet gyönyörű télikert disziti.

Ugy a kávéházban, mint a vendéglőben a legkitűnőbb italok és étkek szo'gáltatnak. Ezenkivül külön berendezett borozó is van szállómban, melyben kül- és belföldi különlegességek kaphatók.

A kiszolgálás a lehető legfigyelmesebb. Társas ebédek, vacsorák, nászlakomák megrendelésre házon kivül is eszközöltetnek.

Ez előkelően berendezett uj szállodámat vőmnek **MENYHÉRT VILMOS** urnak adtam át és igen kérem Czimedet, hogy arra a bizalomra és jóakaratra, mellyel engem kitüntetni méltóztatott, vőmet is érdemesiteni kegyeskedjék.

Mély tisztelettel **idb. RÉMI RÓBERT**
a Nemzeti Szálló volt tulajdonosa.

Vonatkozással az emlitettekre tiszteletteliesan ...
értesitem, hogy a kor ...

Restaurant, 1929 and 1938

Nemzeti Hotel, 1995

HOT

Established: 1912 VI. *Teréz krt.* 43

Britannia Szálloda

HOTEL BÉKE RADISSON

The elegant hotel, converted from an apartment house and fitted with a lift, was opened in 1912 by Henrik Lipót Fábri. Twelve of the rooms had bathrooms and the others hot and cold running water. There was a bathroom on each floor for the use of guests. The restaurant lit with Venetian chandeliers was located in the glass-covered court. The hotel also opened a modern night club and bar.

In 1925 the hotel passed into English ownership. In the following year Aladár Németh, who had previously run the Arany Bika restaurant in Debrecen, was appointed director. In the early 1930s the Szondy bistro was opened in the basement and soon became a popular place among the well-to-do citizenry. Encouraged by the big success, more rooms were opened – Nótás (singer's) Room, Móra Room, Hunter's Room, Székely Bar, Yellow Room – decorated with artistic frescoes, panels and stained glass windows. Many of these were the work of the painter Jenő Haranghy.

In the mid-1930s a coffee-house and espresso lounge were opened and later the first hotel garage in Pest was opened beneath the neighbouring building, with space for 30 cars. 1937 saw the opening of the famous Dome Room with marble fireplaces and a glass dance floor; in the summers the double glass dome could be opened, allowing the public to dance under the sky.

In 1948 the hotel was renamed Béke (Peace) Hotel, and in 1967 it was renovated. Between 1983 and 1985 the hotel was entirely rebuilt, retaining only the original facade and the restored works of art.

Since 1988 the 246-room, four-star hotel has been a member of the Radisson chain.

Brochure, 1933

Restaurant, 1930

Szondy Bistro, 1938

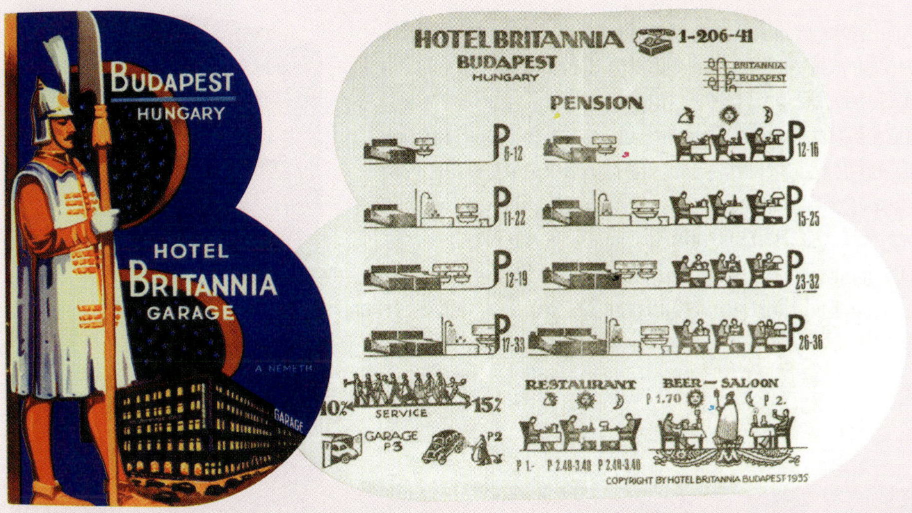

Brochure, 1935

Menu, 1995

Advertisements for the Szondy Bistro, 1938

HOTELS

HOTELS

"I suffered serious hyperacidity and gallstone problems, and learning that there was a dietetic kitchen under excellent medical supervision in the centre of the city, I began to frequent the dietetic restaurant of the Britannia Hotel. The progress is surprising, my pains have disappeared, and on the whole I feel much better. My appetite has increased to the extent that I no longer find the ordinary or large portion sufficient. I can therefore sincerely recommend it to all those who suffer from lack of appetite. The dishes are prepared with a French lightness and are easily digestible. Their appearance too, is important to such sick, nervous persons, as it excites the functioning of the gastric nerves. I repeat, that since I have been frequenting this place I have experienced only recovery, and I warmly recommend the health-restoring art of the Britannia's dietetic kitchen."

Dr. Gy. K., writer on economics

Hotel Béke Radisson, 1995

Established: 1913

V. Apáczai Csere János u. 12–14

Ritz Szálloda

FORUM HOTEL BUDAPEST

The five-storey, 108-room establishment renowned for its elegance and designed by Sándor Fellner was built in 1910 on the site of the Braun restaurant by the Ritz Hotel Co. Its founder was Count Sándor Szapáry who intended this as a demonstration refuting the accusation that the aristocracy was taking its money out of the country. However, the managing director, Madame Ritz, returned home because her child was ill and never came back. She sent a kitchen manager from Paris who ranked above the Hungarian chef, and brought back to Pest two Hungarians who had been working in Paris and were given positions in the Ritz as head waiter and restaurant manager.

In 1916 the Ritz was purchased by the Hungária Grand Hotel Co. which owned the Grand Hotel Hungária, and was renamed the Duna Palace. In 1937 parts of the neighbouring building were joined to the hotel which, this way gained a further 55 rooms.

The luxury hotel was burnt down in 1945. In its place the four-star Forum Hotel Budapest was built in 1981 with Austrian credit. With its multi-storey underground garage, an elegant restaurant, grill, swimming pool, sauna, numerous function rooms and Viennese Coffee Lounge famous for its excellent cakes and pastries, the Forum has become one of Budapest's most popular hotels.

1920s

Restaurant, 1940

Bedroom, 1935 and 1920

HOTELS

Terrace, 1928

HOTELS

"We could tell the story of many long-lived Budapest hotels... but foremost, the story of the Danube Palace which acquired such renown that it even had music dedicated to it.

The piece of music has no title, but the score can be found on page 40 of the issue 27, 1917 of Theatre Life (Színházi Élet), alongside a photograph of the composer.

Judith Harmath

Leaflet from the 1920s

Forum Hotel Budapest, 1995

HOTELS

Established: 1914

V. *Kossuth Lajos u.* 19–21

Astoria Szálloda

The Astoria was built in 1914 according to the plans of Emil Ágoston and Artúr Hikish in Directoire style, on the site of the former Zrínyi inn and coffee-house. Its first leaseholder, Mihály Gellért, returned to Hungary from abroad where he had worked in the famous Waldorf Astoria. Later he was the chief executive officer of the Palatinus Co. on Margaret Island.

The Budapest Astoria gained its present form in the alterations carried out in 1928. It was always a comfortable, elegant, intimate but not extravagant hotel. It was hit by bombs several times during World War II and was unable to receive guests again until 1946. Its bar was a popular night spot.

It was entirely renovated in 1962-63, then again in 1983-86. The 128-room Inner City hotel, located in the centre of the business and commercial district, is a three-star establishment.

Brochure from the 1920s

Foyer, 1920s

Astoria Hotel, 1995

HOTELS

Established: 1918

XI. Szent Gellért tér 1

Szent Gellért Szálloda

GELLÉRT GYÓGYSZÁLLÓ

The Art Nouveau building was designed by Ármin Hegedűs, Artúr Sebestyén and Izidor Sterk on the site of the earlier baths. The elegantly furnished hotel opened in 1918. Its rooms were classified in three categories. The bathrooms in the suites were supplied with normal tap water, thermal water and carbonated water. The medicinal water and modern equipment of the baths attached to the hotel made the Gellért one of Europe's most up-to-date spa hotels.
In the 1920s and 1930s the hotel was further developed, 58 rooms were added, the wave pool was opened in 1927, followed by the indoor carbonated pool in 1933.
The hotel and baths were managed by the municipality, but the restaurants were leased. The first leaseholder was István Frenreisz, followed from 1927 by Károly Gundel who ensured the prestige of the establishments right up to nationalisation. The great master of Hungarian gastronomy greatly increased turnover and under his direction the Gellért cuisine gained an international reputation. Because the Saint Gellért Hotel had the largest catering place in Budapest, able to seat 1500 persons, balls and receptions were often held here.
World War II caused heavy damage to the splendid building. After renovations, the wing overlooking the Danube was reopened in 1961 and the section along Kelenhegyi Road in 1971.
The four-star, 233-room hotel is now used mainly by guests who prefer its dignified elegance, reminiscent of days gone by.

Brochure, 1931

HOTELS

HOTELS

Hall, 1931

Winter garden, 1921

Menu card, 1931

Wine list, 1930s

"In the early 19th century the »filet de boeuf à la Napoleon« was famous. This was a delicious roast of beef they placed in a pigeon, which was stuffed in a chicken, the chicken in a suckling pig, the latter in a turkey, then they carefully roasted the whole, but when it was served only the roast beef was placed on the gourmand's plate. Seeing and enjoying the benefits of tourism, it is the kernel of the many different outer layers and interacting circumstances which hotel-restaurants provide..."

Frigyes Karinthy

"Among others, three of Károly Gundel's famous creations were born in the Gellért: pike-perch in the Rothermere way, mushrooms Bakony style and Pittsburg veal cutlet. But even apart from that, the Gellért is still renowned even abroad for the high standard of its cuisine. To give only one example. Every guest at an international gathering of the industry is a recognised expert. Despite this, Károly Gundel dared to feature goose liver on the menu! This required placing fifty soufflé dishes in hot ovens at precisely the same temperature, all at precisely the same time, so that by the time the consommé cups were removed from the tables the soufflés decorated with slices of goose liver were all served while still fluffy. At a sign, fifty waiters set out with the dishes and another fifty with the bowls of red wine and mushroom sauce. If the timing was out by even a minute, either the guests would have been kept waiting or the soufflé would have collapsed and lost its value. The feat can only be compared to a triple somersault performed blindfold and without a safety net."

Imre Gundel - Judit Harmath:
Memoirs of catering

Hotel Gellért, 1995

SOURCES

page 5
Krúdy Gyula: Pesti vizit (A visit to Pest)
Krúdy Gyula: Régi pesti históriák. (Stories of Old Pest) Magvető, Bp. 1967

page 9
Krúdy Gyula: Pesti vizit (A visit to Pest)
Krúdy Gyula: Régi pesti históriák. (Stories of Old Pest) Magvető, Bp. 1967

page 10
Krúdy Gyula: A nagyétvágyú ember vagy hogyan lakott jól Pátri Pesten.
(The man with an enormous appetite, or how Pátri ate his fill in Pest)
Újság, 28. February 1932

page 11
Gundel Imre – Harmath Judit: A vendéglátás emlékei.
(Memoirs of Catering) *Közgazdasági és Jogi Könyvkiadó, Bp. 1979*

page 13
Lestyán Sándor: Kiskocsmák, nyári zöldvendéglők
(Little inns, summer outdoor restaurants)
Lestyán Sándor: Utazás a fehér asztal körül. (Journey Around the Dinner table)
Közgazdasági és Jogi Könyvkiadó, Bp. 1955

page 14
Szép Ernő (beszéd az Akadémia Szinyei emlékülésén)
(Speech made by Ernő Szép at the Szinyei commemorative session
of the Academy)
Csontváry (Carte Postale)
Herman Lipót: A művészasztal (The Artists' Table)
Képzőművészeti Alap Kiadóvállalata, Bp. 1958

page 16
Bródy István: Ki emlékszik? (Who remembers?)
Bródy István: Régi pesti dáridók. Egy letűnt világ regénye,
(Revelries in Old Pest. Story of a Lost World) Bp. 1940

page 17
Krúdy Gyula: X.Y. pesti demokrata hiteles polgár története
(The Story of X.Y., democrat from Pest and genuine citizen)
Krúdy Gyula: Régi pesti históriák (Stories of Old Pest) Magvető, Bp. 1967

page 18
Bródy István: Hogy mulatnak a mai pestiek? (Entertainment in today's Pest)
Bródy István: Régi pesti dáridók. Egy letűnt világ regénye.
(Revelries in Old Pest. Story of a Lost World) Bp. 1940

page 19
Miss Arizona. Pesti Futár, *1. August 1935*

page 20
Bródy István: A mulatók aranykora (The golden age of bars)
Bródy István: Régi pesti dáridók. Egy letűnt világ regénye.
(Revelries in Old Pest. Story of a Lost World) Bp. 1940

page 21
Bródy István: A mulatók aranykora (The golden age of bars)
Bródy István: Régi pesti dáridók. Egy letűnt világ regénye.
(Revelries in Old Pest. Story of a Lost World) Bp. 1940

page 23
Magyar Elek: Az ínyesmester szakácskönyve (The Gourmet's Cookbook)
Minerva, Bp. 1978

page 25
Heltai Jenő: A Royal-szálló (Hotel Royal) A *Hét, No. 29, 1896*

Hatvany Lajos: A vén kocsmáros és fia, a kontár
(The old innkeeper and his son, the bungler) *Vienna, 1922*

page 27
Bródy Sándor: A pörköltről (On the subject of pörkölt)
A Hét, Political and literary review, 1900–1907, selection, *Magvető, Bp. 1978*

page 29
Galla György: A legrégibb pesti vendéglő. A Százéves Étterem története.
(The oldest restaurant in Pest. History of the Hundred-Year-Old
Restaurant) *Idegenforgalmi Propaganda és Kiadó, Bp. 1987*

page 31
Magyar Elek: Az ínyesmester szakácskönyve (The Gourmet's Cookbook)
Minerva, Bp. 1978

page 32
Mikszáth Kálmán: A magyar konyha – Fecsegés
(Hungarian cuisine – Chatter)
Irodalmi szakácskönyv (Literary Cookbook) Minerva, Bp. 1970

page 34.
A Márvány utca híres vendéglője (The famous restaurant in Márvány Street)
Magyar Kereskedelmi és Vendéglátóipari Múzeum adattára
(Archive of the Museum of Hungarian Commerce and Catering)

page 38
Magyar Elek: Az ínyesmester szakácskönyve (The Gourmet's Cookbook)
Atheneum, Bp. 1932

page 46
Krúdy Gyula: Májusi csodák (May Miracles)
Válogatás Krúdy Gyula gasztronómiai újságcikkeiből.
(Selection from newspaper articles on gastronomy by Gyula Krúdy)
Magyar Kereskedelmi és Vendéglátóipari Múzeum adattára
(Archive of the Museum of Hungarian Commerce and Catering)

page 47
Ruffy Péter: A Gundel család (The Gundel family)
Magyar Nemzet, 16 July 1961

page 49
Móra Ferenc: A költő (The poet)
Móra Ferenc: Napok, holdak, csillagok (Suns, Moons, Stars) Magvető, Bp. 1958
Tömörkény István: Már megint főzünk (Here we go, cooking again)
Irodalmi szakácskönyv (Literary Cookbook) Minerva, Bp. 1970

SOURCES

page 59
Gárdonyi Géza naplója (Diary of Géza Gárdonyi)
Magyar Kereskedelmi és Vendéglátóipari Múzeum gyű jteménye
(Collection of the Museum of Hungarian Commerce and Catering)

page 62
A dunaparti kioszk (The kiosk beside the Danube)
Fővárosi Lapok, 29 May 1889

page 64
Petőfi és más pest-budai polgárok (Petőfi and other citizens of Pest-Buda)
Pest-Budai Petőfi Sándor Emlékház Alapítvány
(Pest-Buda Sándor Petőfi Memorial House Foundation) Bp. 1994

page 65
Gracza György: Az 1848-49-iki szabadságharc története. I. kötet.
(History of the1848-49 War of Independence. Vol. I.)
Lampel Róbert Kiadója, Bp. 1894

page 67
Bródy István: Hogy mulatnak a mai pestiek? (Entertainment in today's Pest)
Bródy István: Régi pesti dáridók. Egy letűnt világ regénye.
(Revelries in Old Pest. Story of a Lost World) Bp. 1940

page 70
Heltai Jenő: A kávéház tündöklése és alkonya
(The flowering and waning of the coffee-house) *Magyar Nap*, 8 May 1949

page 72
Karinthy Frigyes: A pesti pincér (The Pest waiter)
Kávésok Lapja, 30 March 1929

page 74
Gábor Andor: Nehéz leltár (Difficult Inventory)
Szépirodalmi Könyvkiadó, Bp. 1963
Füst Milán
Café Central, az írók kávéháza (Cafe Central, the writers' coffee-house)
Petőfi Irodalmi Múzeum, kiállítási katalógus (Petőfi Literary Museum, exhibition catalogue),1984

page 76
Pest fotográfiája: A Café New-York (Photography of Pest: Café New York).
Színházi Élet, No. 43, 1927

page 77
Gábor Andor
A New-Yorktól a Hungáriáig (From the New York to the Hungária)
Ed.: *Konrádyné Gálos Magda. Minerva*, Bp. 1965
Tarján Vilmos: (t.v.)-től a Tarjánig (From t.v. to Tarján)
Pápai Ernő műintézete, Bp. *no date*

page 79
Kosztolányi Dezső: Cukrász (Confectioner)
Irodalmi Szakácskönyv (Literary Cookbook) Minerva, Bp. 1970

page 81
Szűcs Nándor – Komlós Jenő: Méltóságos cukrászinas
(An aristocratic apprentice confectioner)
Szűcs Nándor – Komlós Jenő: *Pesti háztetők alatt*
(Under the Rooftops of Pest) Published by the authors, Bp. *no date*

page 84
A Gerbeaud titkai (The secrets of the Gerbeaud) *Pesti Futár*, 1910

page 85
Magyar Elek: Az ínyesmester szakácskönyve (The Gourmet's Cookbook)
Minerva, Bp. 1978

page 87
Kosztolányi Dezső: A cukrász (Confectioner)
Irodalmi szakácskönyv (Literary Cookbook) Minerva, Bp. 1970

page 89
Kosztolányi Dezső: Esti Kornél (Kornél Esti)
Kosztolányi Dezső: Összes novellái, 2. *(Collected Novels, Vol. 2)*
Szépirodalmi Könyvkiadó, Bp. 1981

page 92
Krúdy Gyula: Kóczé Anti (Anti Kóczé)
Krúdy Gyula: *Régi pesti históriák (Stories of Old Pest) Magvető*, Bp. 1967

page 93
Takács Lajos: A Hungária Szálloda Pesten (The Hungária Hotel in Pest)
Vasárnapi Újság, 1871

page 98
Császár Ferenc főpincér visszaemlékezése
(Recollections of Ferenc Császár, head waiter)
Tausin Károly: Egy szobapincér elbeszélései (Memoirs of a room waiter)
Történetek a margitszigeti Grand Hotelből (Stories from the Grand Hotel Margaret Island) Pallas Lap- és Könyvkiadó, Bp. 1987

page 108
Dr. F. Gy. közgazdasági író (Dr. Gy. F., writer on economics)
A Britannia Szálloda diaetás konyhája *(The dietic kitchen of Britannia Hotel)*
Korvin testvérek grafikai intézete, Bp. *no date*

page 111
Harmath Judit
Pályázati anyag. Magyar Kereskedelmi és Vendéglátóipari Múzeum adattára
(Project proposal. Archive of the Museum of Hungarian Commerce and Catering)

116. oldal
Karinthy Frigyes
Negyven év a magyar szállodás- és vendéglősipar életéből (1891-1931)
(Forty years in the life of the Hungarian hotel and restaurant industry)
Eds.: *Károly Ballai and Kornél Tábori*, Bp. 1936

117. oldal
Gundel Imre – Harmath Judit: A vendéglátás emlékei
(Memoirs of Catering) *Közgazdasági és Jogi Könyvkiadó*, Bp. 1979

ZÁRVA
GESCHLOSSEN
CLOSED